LIFE LESSONS II

Learned From Sports

BY JOHN ED MATHISON

WELCOME!

"I would like to welcome you to our Leadership Ministries
and outreach! Our vision is one of - **Hope, Inspiration, Challenge**
and **Love.** We offer you multiple ways to receive this Ministry:
We offer you multiple ways to receive this Ministry: Our Daily
Message and Weekly Blog, our Daily Radio Message, our Weekly Videos, and our monthly Go Getters & Go Givers Podcast.
We invite you to pray for opportunities to share in our vision
and return often! Your support is greatly appreciated."

—JOHN ED

READ | LISTEN | WATCH

Visit: johnedmathison.org

LIFE LESSONS II

Learned From Sports

I've always loved sports. In my early years, I enjoyed listening to baseball games on the radio with my Dad. I grew up in Opelika, Alabama so I was able to go to a lot of sporting events in Auburn. When we got a television, I thought I had gone to heaven.

I played basketball, football, and tennis in high school. Basketball afforded me a full scholarship to go through college at Young Harris Junior College and Huntingdon College. I also played #1 singles in tennis for four years in college and never lost a match.

Following college, I played basketball with the Venture for Victory team. We played multiple games against the Olympic teams in Asia. The Philippine team was the defending Asia Games champion. We played them four times to capacity crowds in the 17,000 seat Araneta Coliseum in Manilla. We also played several games against Olympic teams in Japan, Korea, Taiwan, and Hong Kong. We played 66 other games against colleges and communities in ten weeks. We only lost eight games all summer. Winning attracted more people to the games and gave added credibility to our witness.

At halftime we had 15 minutes to give a Christian witness and challenge. We saw thousands of people sign up for a Bible correspondence course as they made decisions for Jesus Christ. Venture for Victory was the forerunner to Athletes in Action programs which expanded to include baseball, soccer, etc.

I played competitive tennis, racket ball, and pickleball. I served on the Governor's Council on Physical Fitness, and I served on the National Board of Fellowship of Christian Athletes. I've done team devotions for multiple college and high school teams. I've spoken at many coaches' conferences and FCA events.

There are fifty-two lessons in this book-one for every week of the year. Many people will use it for Sunday School lessons, school lessons, personal enrichment, and many other ways. Some businesspeople buy a copy for each of their employees. Some school systems will buy a book for each of their coaches. Some coaches will buy a book for each of their team members. I firmly believe that any athlete is a better athlete when he or she becomes a better person.

We have one full page of Quotable Quotes. A friend said that the quotes are worth the price of the book.

Books can be ordered from our ministry office at 4135 Carmichael Road, Suite 3000, Montgomery, Alabama, 36106. The cost is $10.00 per book plus postage. Books can be purchased at Henig Furs, Adams Drugs, the Locker Room, Frazer bookstore, and Mathison Interiors in Auburn.

Join me in practicing these life lessons learned from sports!!

TABLE OF

Contents

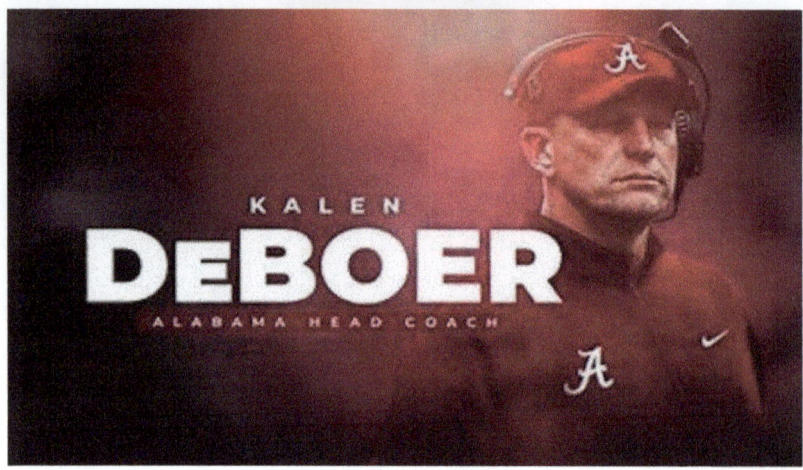

GRAWLIX

The University of Alabama has a new football coach following the retirement of Nick Saban. His name is Kalen DeBoer. He has a great resume and has been highly successful. He led Washington to a second-place finish in the football polls this year. He has a good personality. He is outgoing. He has made a favorable hit with Alabama fans.

There is one thing that I really like about him that has caused so much interest in sports talk radio concerning the coach. He doesn't cuss. He is proud of the fact that he doesn't cuss.

Many people have replied that cussing is just a part of the vocabulary of being a coach. I disagree tremendously with that. I played sports at Opelika High School, and I never heard my coach Sam Mason cuss. I played basketball at Young Harris Junior College under Luke Rushton and never heard him cuss. I played basketball at Huntingdon College under Coach Neal Posey and never heard him cuss. I have had a lot of people tell me that they are playing for coaches today who don't cuss.

Don't be fooled by Satan's lie that it's okay to cuss-everybody does it. Everybody doesn't do it! Cussing and living a Christian witness are incompatible.

Your language identifies you. It happened to Peter. When people heard him speak, his language identified where he was from, and he was accused of being a follower of Jesus. (Matthew 26:73-74) After seminary, I went to

Princeton to get another graduate degree. People there quickly picked up on my accent and identified where I was from. I rather enjoyed it because people would offer to buy my lunch if I would just talk. I put on a little extra southern drawl in order to give them their money's worth. Cussing or not cussing identifies who you are!

I have had people tell me that they feel uncomfortable around me because they cuss. They should be uncomfortable because they report to God, not me, and God is around them everywhere they go!

Jesus said, "Whatever you have said in the dark will be heard in the light." (Luke 12:3) Paul said, "Let no unwholesome word proceed out of your mouth." (Ephesians 4:29)

Many people tell me that they cannot stop cussing. They say it's their "cross to bear." It is not their cross to bear-it's our cross to bear. It's their choice to use words that are offensive to God and to people.

Some people ask me how they can stop cussing. **HERE'S HOW:** (1) Decide to quit. (2) Ask God to hold you accountable. (3) Tell your family and a trusted Christian friend that you are going to quit. (4) Tell then that every time you use a cuss word, you will write a $100 check to your church or to some ministry. I guarantee this process: If you follow these four steps and don't quit, I'll write you a $100 check!

If you have trouble cussing when you send a message on your computer, there is a new word known as GRAWLIX. You spell it by using the symbols! @#$%&* instead of the cuss word.

Discuss this topic when you have lunch with friends or find yourself in any group. Help start a new wave of language that is helpful and supportive and encouraging to all people. You will be blessed-and you will bless others around you.

Thanks Coach DeBoer. You are already a winner in my book!

LIFE LESSON

LANGUAGE IS IMPORTANT

#1 LESSONS FROM A #1 GOLFER!

On Sunday, April 14, 2024, the number one golf tournament in the world, The Masters, put the green jacket on Scottie Scheffler again. I predict he will have a closet full of green jackets soon.

He is a great teacher. We can learn from the best. Here are some of his real golf lessons:

1. Scottie Scheffler is number one in the golf world-but the golf world is not number one in him! His priority is his commitment to Jesus Christ. Golf is a platform that he uses to share his faith. He makes it clear that golf is what he does-it is not his identity. His identity is that he is a follower of Jesus. His security and confidence are the cross and resurrection of Jesus.

2. His second priority is to be a Godly husband. His wife Meredith was pregnant with their first child and her due date was sometimes around the Masters event. He told everyone at the Masters that if his wife went into labor, he would withdraw from the competition and go to be with her. Think about that. How many people who are knocking on the door of $3.6 million and the number one golf ranking in the world would give all of that up just to be with their wife when their child is born? What if he had received a phone call early Sunday morning when he was ready to play the final round? I know what he would have done. What would you have done?

3. He knows the value of surrounding himself with strong Christian friends. He met eHHHHH Ted Scott in a Bible study, and they became accountability partners. Ted became his caddie. I was touched by the scene when he sank the last putt on the 18th green. He embraced Ted. Walking up to sign his score card, a lot of people stopped Ted to congratulate him. Scheffler stopped and waited for him to catch up so they could walk to the victory table together.

4. Scheffler commented on how during the week he knew how much he wanted to win. He confessed that he hated to lose. He was with some of his friends and expressed how he was struggling. The group reminded him that his security was not on the golf course but was in the cross of Jesus Christ. Scheffler said that when he heard that, it made all the difference. He knew where his real security was deposited. Where is your security?

5. He was one of the most focused athletes I've seen. He wasn't going to be distracted. Paul wrote, "This one thing I do, forgetting what's behind and reaching for what is front of me, I press on toward the goal of the prize of the high calling of God in Jesus Christ" (Philippians 3:14) To me, that's Scottie Scheffler.

Quiz time: What is your #1 priority? Are your friends a Godly influence? To whom are you accountable? Would you be driving the same car if you made $54 million in your job? Who gets the glory when you win? Are your answers to these questions the same as Sheffler's answers would be?

Three points to memorize: Winning the Masters is not as important as knowing Jesus Christ as your Master. The Masters' $3.6 million prize doesn't compare to The Master's promise of heavenly riches! The Masters' victory will only be in the history books, but the victory of placing your security and identity in the The Master puts your name in the Lamb's Book of Life!

Homework: Share this blog with your golf friends (and others).

LIFE LESSON

PUTTING PRORITIES IN PLACE

7

A VISIT I'LL NEVER FORGET!

When I finished college, I was invited to play basketball on the Venture for Victory Basketball Team, which traveled throughout Asian countries, playing basketball, and presenting a Christian witness. We played about 75 games in ten weeks. Several of them were against Olympic teams from Japan, Taiwan, Korea, Philippines, and Hong Kong. Thousands of people came to know Christ through that program.

One of my most unforgettable life experiences occurred in Taipei. We were playing each night against their Olympic team. Some missionaries invited us to visit a leprosarium that was run by Mrs. Lillian Dickson. She was a marvelous Presbyterian lady who had a remarkable ministry to lepers.

Basketball is really big in that part of the world. Even the leprosarium had a basketball court. It also had loud-speakers throughout the compound so that people could listen to the ball games. We gave a basketball demonstration at the court. Some of the residents not too badly affected by leprosy were able to walk to the court. Others brought their buddies on their backs.

We saw how leprosy affected people at different stages. Some were severely afflicted, while others were in the first stages. I met a man named Chhoe who had been a skilled wood carver. Leprosy took his fingers, so he strapped the chisel to the heel of one hand and the mallet to the heel of his other hand, and carved water buffaloes. He gave me one.

Mrs. Dickson invited us to go to the top of the compound to what she called the "ward nearest heaven." The most severely afflicted lepers were there. There were eight lepers in the room. None of them had arms or feet. Someone had to feed them and care for them. It was a dimly lit room. None of these lepers would live very long, but the remarkable thing was that each of them had accepted Jesus Christ as their Savior. They knew the real meaning of life, and their lives were effervescent with the hope of eternity.

I have been in a lot of prayer groups and religious settings in my life. Never had I been in any room where I felt the power of God so much as in that leprosarium. Mrs. Dickson called on one of our players to lead in prayer. Gary Cunningham, All-American basketball player from UCLA, began to pray, with the use of an interpreter, "Oh God, we thank you for Jesus Christ."

All-of-a-sudden, the lepers started saying in English, "Hallelujah, hallelujah. Amen, amen." They started praising God. Gary was unable to continue the prayer. It was just an outbreak of genuine praise to God.

Mrs. Dickson took us outside and explained that when Gary thanked God for Jesus Christ, he thanked God for the only hope those men had. Their focus was not on a basketball game, or earning money, or trying to establish a vocation-none of these were important at all to these lepers. Knowing Jesus and where they would spend eternity was the greatest news they could hear and share!

My life would never be the same after that experience. Today, what are you most thankful for? Where is your hope? What do you love more than anything else in the world? In what are you putting your trust? What is your focus in life today?

Learn from these lepers about real living!

LIFE LESSON

PRAISE GOD IN ALL STUATIONS

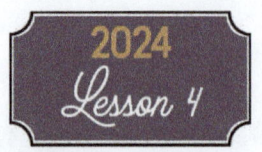

DWJD

Brett Butler was a great baseball player. In the 1990s, he went in for a tonsillectomy, but discovered that there was also a malignant cancer involved. He had surgery and chemotherapy.

He was traded to the Los Angeles Dodgers, then to the Atlanta Braves. He worked hard to come back from his cancer surgery. At his first appearance on the field in Atlanta, he was given a five-minute standing ovation. He then developed other complications.

He was on one of the late night tv talk shows and was asked about his cancer, but he preferred to talk about his faith. He told how he walked into his daughter's bedroom as she was saying her prayers. She didn't know he was standing there, and in glow of the nightlight, he saw her diligently talking about her daddy and what a great influence her daddy was to so many people and how she was asking God to heal him because of all the good that he does.

Brett Butler said he could see tears coming down her cheeks. Then he heard her say, "God, please let me have his cancer so he can live, and he can do so much more for people than I ever could." Brett Butler saw in his little daughter somebody who was more interested in his life than her own life. That's DWJD- doing what Jesus did!

What if the whole world had that attitude about life? I had a life-defining experience one Sunday. During my sermon, which was carried on television,

I talked about how Jesus died for us. I then made the statement that I couldn't think of anybody outside my family who would literally die for me.

That afternoon I received a phone call from Dr. Chip Armstrong, one of Alabama's best surgeons. Chip and I have done a lot together in the Fellowship of Christian Athletes settings. He said, "John Ed, I heard you on television this morning. You are wrong. I would gladly die in your place if I had to make that choice."

Wow! A medical doctor who was not even a member of my church or my denomination would do that for me. His call both encouraged and challenged me. I will never forget it. That's DWJD.

A group of people were discussing the question, "What is your favorite football game?" Different people offered different opinions. A retired Navy Seal said that his favorite football game is the Army-Navy game. I was intrigued by that answer because my grandson, David Hixon, played football at the Naval Academy, and played in that game.

Someone asked the Navy Seal why that was his favorite game. He said, "It's simple. It's the only football game in which every player on the field is willing to die for every person in the stands." Wow! That's a different look at football and life! That's DWJD.

I love it when I hear people thank military persons for their service. I always try to do that. Many of them often respond with a simple statement, "Thank you. Let's make this a nation worth dying for." Amen!

Our nation needs people who are willing to love all people unconditionally like God has loved us. Jesus said, "Greater love has no man than this that a man would give his life for another person." (John 16:13) That's what Jesus did.

I love you this much a child would say, and throw his arms out wide. So, Jesus grew up to love that way, and with outstretched arms He died!

Are we willing to DWJD-do what Jesus did?

LIFE LESSON

ALWAYS FOLLOW JESUS

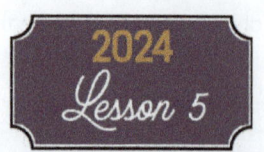

THINK ABOUT IT!

When you wake up every morning, you decide what your day is going to be like. The Bible says, "As man thinks in his heart, so is he." (Proverbs 23:7) Your thinking determines your actions. So, your first thoughts are extremely important.

While speaking in Arkansas, I met an outstanding man who has been one of the leading salespersons in the State of Arkansas. He has received daily the things I write and shared some of them with his two performance coaches, Tom Bartow and Dr. Jason Selk.

These two performance coaches are extremely successful in coaching Fortune 500 and Fortune 100 company executives, Olympic and college athletes, and professional athletic teams. You can Google both of them and read about their impressive list of clients and accomplishments.

I met a financial advisor in Alabama recently who is a client of these performance coaches and asked him to evaluate their work. He said, "I have been a client of theirs for two years and in that time, my sales have increased 43%. They focus on continual improvement.

I've had several phone conversations with them about how they could add a ministry arm to their work to give back to churches to help them become more effective. They want to share their success.

They write and teach a very interesting concept of how our thinking not only determines what we do but is highly influenced physiologically. Here is a very brief summary.

They teach that if you focus on problems, your brain releases into your blood stream the neurotransmitter known as Cortisol. This can be really bad because Cortisol is the root of negative emotions. They say that humans do not have the ability to experience negative emotions such as fear, anger, and stress without the release of Cortisol into the blood stream.

Cortisol decreases cognitive functioning. People who start the day with negative thoughts of what can't be done release elevated levels of Cortisol causing them to be stressed out, unaware of how to correct the issues. Some of the extreme results are road rage, anger, shootings, and suicide.

But there is good news. When people focus on positive solutions, the brain stops releasing Cortisol and begins releasing a new set of neurotransmitters-dopamine, serotonin, and norepinephrine. These neurotransmitters biologically cause a person to feel happy and motivated and the person will have measurable increases in intelligence, creativity, energy, and positive results.

Dr. Selk treats this concept extensively in his book, Relentless Solution Focus. The subtitle is "how to train your mind to conquer stress, pressure, and underperformance."

So, you see you choose your thoughts, and they release into your blood stream either bad or good neurotransmitters which will determine your actions, which will determine your day. What kind of day you have is not based on circumstances or other people. It is based on your thinking and your actions.

Begin each day with Psalm 118:24. "This is the day the Lord has made. Let us rejoice and be glad in it." Then during the day, follow Paul's advice to "guard your heart and your mind and focus on what is true, honorable, right, pure, lovely, of good report. Let your mind dwell on these things" (Philippians 4:7,8)

What kind of day are you having?

LIFE LESSON

WHAT ARE YOU THINKING?

MISTAKEN IDENTITY

Occasionally somebody confuses a person with someone else that they have seen or heard about. That happened to me three times in one day recently. Each mistaken identity was a compliment.

The Camelia Bowl is one of the more popular bowls carried by ESPN. I serve on the River Region Sports Commission, and we sponsor that bowl and the activities connected with it. One of the activities is a huge luncheon at the Renaissance honoring the football teams, their fans, and some Legend.

Dr. James Andrews was selected as the Legend to honor at this year's Camelia Bowl. As you probably know, he is an orthopedic surgeon and has operated on more professional athletes in every sport than probably anybody else. I have been in his office complex in Birmingham and it is covered with pictures of great athletes who have thanked him for operating on them.

I was amazed to learn that he is on the sidelines for most all of the Auburn, Alabama, UAB, and Troy football games. His beautiful wife was present, and he thanked her for going with him. He said that last year, she attended 55 football games with him!

The next day following the legends banquet, I was on the sidelines for the game with my granddaughter, Healey Mathison. One of the coaches came up to me before the game and said, "Could I have my picture made with you?" I looked around because I figured one of my friends was playing a trick on me, but didn't see anybody.

As he had someone taking our picture, he said, "Can I ask you a couple of questions?" I said, "Sure." He said, "Tell me about the new techniques you are using in doing knee surgeries and particularly shoulder surgeries." I quickly realized that he had seen me talking with Dr. Andrews and had me confused with him. I told him who I was, and he was very nice but quickly knew that he had a mistaken identity.

A few minutes later another person came up to me and said, "Could I have my picture made with you?" Again, I looked to see if one of my friends was playing a trick on me. This person introduced herself as the assistant athletic director at her college and said that she was impressed by my speech at the Legend's Luncheon when I talked about the importance of academics as well as athletics. I realized she had me confused with the Commissioner of her athletic conference who I remembered making those statements. I again was glad to be mistaken for the commissioner.

When I left the ballgame, I stopped by Publix grocery store. As I was walking down the aisle, an older African American gentleman looked at me and said, "Thank you for your service." I was wearing a Navy cap that had been given to me by my grandson who played football at the Naval Academy. Again, I looked around because I was sure somebody was playing a trick on me. I thanked him for thanking me for my service, but told him I hadn't actually served in the armed forces. He looked at me with a puzzled look and said, "Oh, I saw your cap and I looked at you and thought you must have been a Navy Seal."

Imagine my being mistaken for a Navy Seal! I wear that Navy cap a lot today!

When people see you and think you are a Christian-are they right or mistaken? Paul said, "It is no longer I who live, but it is Christ who lives in me." (Galatians 2:20) Anyone who belongs to Christ is a new person. The old life is gone, and a new life has begun. (II Corinthians 5:17)

When people see you, who do they see?

LIFE LESSON

IDENTIFY YOURSELF

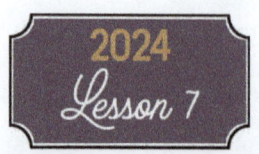

REMEMBER TO FORGET

On April 3, 1989, Michigan was playing Seton Hall for the NCAA men's basketball national championship. The game came down to the final second when a Michigan guard by the name of Rumeal Robinson drove for the basket and was fouled while shooting.

Michigan was behind one point. He had two foul shots with one second left. If he makes the foul shots Michigan wins; if he misses, they lose.

About two weeks before that, Michigan had played a game against Wisconsin. It was the same scenario when Robinson drove for the basket with Michigan trailing by one point. He was fouled and missed both foul shots and Michigan lost that game.

Seton Hall called time out. A couple of the players walked by Robinson going to the bench and said, "Remember Wisconsin, remember Wisconsin." Some hecklers behind the Michigan bench were yelling, "Remember Wisconsin, remember Wisconsin." Robinson went out and calmly sank the two foul shots and Michigan won their first national championship, 80-79.

When asked how he got it out of his mind what had happened in Wisconsin, he said, "I learned from that never to look back. Forget it!! was only looking forward to making two shots that would win for us a national championship." You can either look back or look forward-it's your choice.

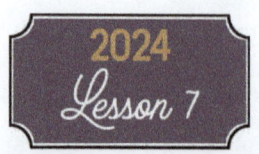

16

Learning to forget is a valuable talent. We've all had things in the past that would hinder us from going forward in the future. If we continue to dwell on those things, we will ruin our future. Yesterday might have been a disappointment, but don't dwell on yesterday. The earth has made a complete circle around the sun since yesterday. Forget it and look forward to this new day and its possibilities.

Dr. John Claypool tells about his grandfather who lived in southern Kentucky on a farm. Six generations of his family lived there. They had an orchard, and one day the wind blew down an old pear tree that had been there as long as anybody could remember. Claypool said that his grandfather was grieved to lose the tree because he had both played on it as a young boy and had eaten fruit from it all of his life.

A neighbor came by and said to his grandfather, "I am really sorry to see your pear tree blown down." His grandfather replied, "I am sorry too. It was a real part of my past."

The neighbor then inquired, "What are you going to do?" His grandfather paused and thought for a minute and said, "I am going to pick the fruit and burn what's left."

That's a good way to live. Pick the fruit, but burn what's left.

Clara Barton founded the American Red Cross. One day a friend was asking her something about her past when she had been mistreated. When she ignored the comment, her friend said, "Don't you remember that?" Clara Barton replied, "No, I don't remember it. I distinctly remember forgetting it."

Forgetting what needs to be forgotten is not a sign of old age. It is a sign of a new age that God is giving us. It's a sign that we can forget what we need to forget, then do what needs to be done. Paul said to forget what is behind you, reach forward to what is in front of you, and move towards the prize of fulfilling God's purpose for you. (Philippians 3:13-14)

It's time to remember what to forget!

LIFE LESSON

A MEMORY STRATEGY

MOUNTAIN TOPS AND VALLEYS

Sometimes in life we feel like we are living on a mountaintop. Other times, we feel like we are in the valley. Paul said that we ought to be thankful in all situations of life. (Ephesians 5:20; I Thessalonians 5:18)

One of the best examples of this is Coach Jimmy Perry. About thirty years ago, he was one of the top weightlifters in the state and was a runner up to the Mr. Alabama contest. He then discovered he had to have a kidney transplant.

I went to Birmingham with him. His faith was radiant! The transplant was successful.

Last November, as he and his wife, Judy, were driving to Birmingham for a check-up, they received a phone call from the Alabama High School Athletic Association congratulating him on being selected to the Alabama Football Coaches Hall of Fame. He was on the mountaintop.

Later that day in the doctor's office, the examination revealed clear cell cancer. They told him that he only had less than three months to live.

From the mountaintop to the valley. It was a long drive back home. But Jimmy has a strong faith, a great attitude, and a lot of people praying for him.

Thanksgiving and Christmas of 2021 were really tough as Jimmy processed the fact that this would be the last ones he would spend with his wife, kids, and grandkids. His faith was strong.

He and Judy went back to Birmingham for his final check-up in January 2022. His doctors were immediately amazed because they couldn't find the cancer! The doctor asked him what he had been doing. Jimmy replied, "We have been praying." The doctor's reply was, "What you're doing is working a whole lot better than what we are doing."

The doctor then said we have one more test we need to run involving your DNA. He said there's only a one percent chance that this test will prove that you are clear. Jimmy looked at him and smiled and said, "One percent and God is all the odds I need." Jimmy was right. The test showed complete healing!

As usual in August, he invited me to come over and speak to his football team and their parents at the beginning of the season and have a prayer in the locker room for the families.

The picture above shows us with his quarterback, K.J. Jackson. He is a big boy. I offered to give K.J. a few tips of playing quarterback, but Jimmy wisely said we didn't have time!

Saint James had its best season ever. They played Piedmont, the defending state champions, in the Championship game and were trailing 20-10 at the half. Jimmy and his staff made adjustments at halftime and came out and scored 35 points and won 45-28!

K.J. threw for 5 touchdowns in the second half and was the MVP. He is only a junior and had 41 touchdown passes for the year!

Coach Perry was back on the mountaintop, but he lives as humbly and gratefully on the mountaintop as he does in the valley. He believes in the power of healing. He has experienced it. He still makes every day count. He still wants to make a difference in the lives of young people.

How do you handle the mountaintops and the valleys?

LIFE LESSON

HOW TO BE A REAL WINNER

WHO REALLY WON?

College football has become big business. The introduction of the NIL Name Image Likeness-has made it possible for players to get paid huge amounts of money. Some college players are making well over $1 million a year.

The introduction of the Transfer Portal has also revolutionized football. If you have a good NIL program, you can get a lot of players out of the transfer portal who add tremendously to your team. Signing on recruiting day is still important, but so many of those high-round recruits wind up at another school.

The buy-out for head coaches in the SEC, who get fired, has become one of the most lucrative professions anywhere. Someone said that if you can ever get a head coaching job, you will be set for life.

Auburn had a coaching change on November 1. It was a culmination of a lot of discussion over the last couple of years. The fired coach Bryan Harsin should be able to live on the buy-out!

An interim coach was named the next day. It was Carnell "Cadillac" Williams. He is a former great running back. He was the coach for the running backs for Auburn this year.

Cadillac is a breath of fresh air for college football. He came in with energy and enthusiasm. He had no experience as a head coach, and only four days to prepare for Mississippi State. Five of the assistant coaches had also been fired. With little time to prepare, Auburn went into the game with an inexperienced head coach and an offensive line coach in charge of calling the plays. No wonder Auburn was a big underdog.

But Cadillac did not dwell on how bad the situation was. He began by thanking God for the opportunity he was given. His enthusiasm and energy were contagious. Auburn almost upset Mississippi State. They lost in overtime.

But did they really lose? They did on the scoreboard, but in the postgame conference, Coach Williams talked about the Chapel service for the team on Friday night. I've had the opportunity to speak at that service. The FCA Chaplain at Auburn is my good friend, Chette Williams. He and Coach Williams have more in common than the same last name and the same initials-they have the same values about winning.

In the Chapel Service on Friday night, Coach Williams reported that eight football players accepted Jesus Christ as their personal savior! Wow! Coach Williams was excited about that. In my opinion, that's the most important thing a coach can do. In the future, people will forget the score of the game, but for eternity people will remember the win that night in the Chapel service.

I don't know how the future will go with Coach Williams, but he has certainly injected a great perspective that I think that all coaches should follow.

The question for you and me is what kind of energy, discipline, teamwork, and "never quit attitude" do we bring to our work every day? Is our job a platform for doing ministry? I recognize there are some HR guidelines that have to be followed, but within those how can I win people to faith in Jesus Christ?

Football at Auburn is different-and eight young men are really different!

LIFE LESSON

KNOW WHEN YOU ARE REALLY WINNING

HERE COMES THE JUDGE

The baseball world was focused on the second game of the Yankees Series with the Rangers. The 38,832 people made it the largest paid attendance in Globe Life Field's two-year history. This was next to the last opportunity for Aaron Judge to break the American League home run record held by Roger Maris.

Interestingly, it was the third pitch by the Ranger's pitcher, Jesus Tino That's right, his name was Jesus Tinoco. It was a slider clocked at 884 miles an hour. He connected with the pitch, and it ended up 391 feet away in section 31, row 1, seat 3. It was caught by a Dallas resident Corey Youmans. The ball is reportedly worth more than $4 million!

Roger Maris, Jr. was in the stands. His dad had held the record for years. He complimented Judge by saying he was glad that a man of his character and integrity broke his dad's record.

There is a section in Yankee Stadium that fans refer to as the Courtroom. They wear black robes. When Aaron Judge comes up to bat, they start chanting, "Here comes the Judge" and "All rise. Yankee Stadium comes alive. Aaron Judge then gives them even more to cheer about.

Aaron Judge is a class Christian gentleman. He stands 6 feet 7 inches tall and weighs 282 pounds. He's a big man, but he is even bigger in terms of his faith in Jesus Christ.

When asked how he handled the stress of the last few games of the season, he said he did it by trying to take one day at a time and to pray a lot. He always commented about how much prayer and his relationship to Jesus Christ meant in his career.

Judge was carrying a copy of II Corinthians 5:7 in his pocket when he broke the record. He said, "It's one of my favorite bible verses. I try to live my life by it and always trust the Man above and what He's got in store for us. We never know what's around the corner, but if we have faith in Him, He will guide us in the right direction." What's in your pocket?

Last year, he married his high school sweetheart. In today's world, it's good to see a couple who love each other, not because of the success of one of them, but because of their long-term commitment to Jesus Christ and to each other. He and his wife are doing so many things together to enhance the lives of many, many people.

He was adopted and his parents never told him until he was ten years old. Judge is a great reason to oppose abortion. He said that God really blessed him with such supportive parents. They try to stay out of the limelight.

I love reading about Aaron Judge. May God increase his tribe. I hope you will share with a lot of high school and little league baseball players the real values of Aaron Judge.

When asked about his priorities, he quickly said, "My Christian faith, my family, and baseball." He knows what's most important in life.

I like his attitude of constantly improving. He said recently. "If what you did yesterday still seems big today, then you haven't done anything today."

What are you doing today?

LIFE LESSON

BE A GOOD JUDGE

COACHES AND PLAYERS SPEAK UP

I am inspired when I hear coaches and athletes speak up publicly about their Christian faith. I've read that % of the starting quarterbacks in the NFL are professing Christians. Sports provides a platform to share their faith. Here are a few examples:

Patrick Mahomes quarterbacked his team to the Super Bowl. After the AFC Championship game, Mahomes said, "I just want to thank God. He healed my body this week. Faith is always a big part of what I do. It helps you know why you are playing the game and who you're doing it for.

Jalen Hurts quarterbacked his team to the Super Bowl. After the NFC Championship game, he said, "Only God knows the things that each individual on this team has been able to overcome to come together as a team and do something special. My favorite Bible verse has sustained me when I went through a lot of stuff in college, and it kind of stuck with me, John 13:7 'You may not know now, but later you'll understand."

Brock Purdy was the last player chosen in the NFL draft last year, number 259. Because of injuries to the quarterbacks of San Francisco, he wound up being the starter. He won his first seven games before he was injured in the Championship game. He said, "My identity is in Jesus Christ. I love playing football, but football is just a game. I identify as a Christian before I identify as a football player!"

Frank Reich was just named the head football coach of the Charlotte Panthers. He is a former pastor. (Maybe I can go into coaching.) He sees coaching as a larger platform to do ministry. He says, "At the end of the day, I just want to be faithful to exalt the name of Christ, be faithful to live out, eat, breathe, and sleep the Word of God. That is my focus."

Roberto Firmino plays a different kind of football (soccer) which is the most popular sport in the world. The star from Liverpool became a Christian three years ago because of the witness of his teammates and competitors. He speaks in churches on Sundays.

Jacie Hoyt is the Oklahoma State women's basketball coach. She said, "Three things make my world go round...Jesus, family, hoops. I feel such a strong sense of purpose every day that I wake up to just get to go and live the way that I think Jesus wants me to live, and that He would live."

Chanda Rigby, head women's basketball coach at Troy University, has put women's basketball on the map at Troy. I speak at a FCA Coaches Conference every June, and she and her football coach husband and family are always there. I have heard her say, "Basketball and sports are important, but knowing Jesus Christ is the most important thing in life."

Bruce Pearl is head basketball coach at Auburn. He recently gave the following note to his team and staff: "Pray for blessings from God so that we can bless others. Pray for influence so that we can minister and do more. Pray that God would put his hand on us. Pray for God's anointing like he anointed Moses. We have to have His blessing and his anointing to do all we can do. Our competence comes from God, not us. Lord knows it's true of me. Thank you for overcoming my weaknesses and inabilities. But I know God's got us! Have a blessed Sunday."

How are you using your situation in your life today to share the Good News of Christ?

LIFE LESSON

IT'S TIME TO SPEAK UP

2024
Lesson 12

UNDERRATED TO OVERCOMER!

He came out of high school, and no big colleges were interested in him. He wasn't fast enough, big enough, or talented enough. He was just a skinny kid about six feet tall and 170 pounds and played football in an area that wasn't known for great competition. Only two small schools from the FCS offered him a scholarship. He accepted one to Eastern Washington.

When he came out of college, not many pro teams were interested in him. He was underrated and overlooked, but the Los Angeles Rams took a chance and drafted him. Wow, what a great move!

In the 2021 football season, he was the best receiver in the NFL. He achieved the triple crown of catches (145), touchdown catches (16), and receiving yards (1947). In the Super Bowl, he led a last-minute comeback by catching multiple passes despite double coverage. He caught the winning touchdown pass with just over a minute to go. He was voted the most valuable player in Super Bowl LVI!

He is a strong Christian. He places Bible verses on his helmet and his sleeve. He always gives a Christian witness when being interviewed. When asked about his Super Bowl ring, he said that, as a Christian, he wanted to win in the game of life where he would receive a trophy that would never perish.

Look what God can do! God took Cooper Kupp from an underrated and overlooked player to the best player on the biggest stage in pro football, and Cooper gives God all the credit.

Last year, Zaila Avant-garde became the first Black American to win the Scripps National Spelling Bee. She is not just a great speller, but she also holds three Guinness World Records for basketball. Zaila dribbled simultaneously the most basketballs (six for 30 seconds), the most basketball bounces (307 in 30 seconds), and the most bounce juggles in 1 minute (255 with four basketballs).

A lot of people said she couldn't do much. She was underrated but became an overcomer. She excelled beyond people's expectations.

One of my favorite basketball players is Steph Curry. He is always inspiring people who have felt overlooked, unappreciated, and underrated. Steph Curry was a 3-star recruit, considered the #52 high school point guard in the country, and attended Davidson after being turned down by all the top college programs.

But Curry refused to see himself as underrated. He has a strong Christian faith. He believed God saw him as an overcomer and helped him develop an elite positive attitude about shooting a basketball.

Curry has risen to a level where he is considered the greatest shooter in basketball history. On December 14, 2021, the Warriors were playing the New York Knicks. With 7:33 remaining in the first quarter of the game, Curry hit a 3 pointer which broke Ray Allen's all-time 3-point field goal record of 2,973. He set a record that people think will never be broken. And he still has a lot of games to play!

Steph Curry has a strong faith and believes that nobody should accept less than what God created them to be. There is no room for excuses. You can't listen to all the people who tell you what you can't do. Listen to God and learn what He can do through you!

God delights in turning the underrated into overcomers!

LIFE LESSON

DON'T UNDERESTIMATE POTENTIAL

WHY YOU DO WHAT YOU DO

Baseball in 2022 has seen records shattered and unbelievable accomplishments achieved. One player enhanced his future Hall of Fame resume. He did something great for baseball, but the reason he did it is what makes him special.

Albert Pujols plays for the St. Louis Cardinals. He is 42 years old and is supposed to be "over-the-hill," but he is setting a new hill, and doing it for the greatest reason in the world.

Only three other players have hit 700 home runs in their careers-Babe Ruth, Barry Bonds, and Hank Aaron. Albert Pujols hit his 700th home run on September 23, 2022. He has since hit a few more this season. Also, he is one of only two players who has had 3,000 hits during his career!

People are amazed at his performance. As one of his coaches said, "He's hitting home runs in the major leagues against young kids that nowadays are throwing every pitch 95 to 100 mph, and he's catching up to it like it's no big deal. He's the best hitter in the major leagues against left-handed pitching!"

Pujols has made it very clear that his life is not about baseball records but about introducing people to Jesus Christ. He says, "I've heard kids say that they want to be just like me when they grow up. They should know that I want to be like Jesus."

He uses his baseball career as a platform to witness for Christ. He once said, "My life goal is to bring glory to Jesus. My life is not mostly dedicated to the Lord; it is 100% committed to Jesus Christ and His will. God has given me the ability to succeed in the game of baseball, but baseball is not the end. Baseball is a means by which my wife, Dee Dee, and I glorify God. Baseball is simply my platform to elevate Jesus Christ, my Lord and my Savior."

Pujols and his wife have a foundation which serves children and families impacted by Down Syndrome. He also serves many impoverished people in the Dominican Republic.

Pujols states emphatically that baseball is not his chief ambition in life. He says, "Becoming a great baseball player is important to me, but it's not my primary focus because I know the Hall of Fame is not my ultimate final destination."

Wow-I love a man who has excelled in his sport and who has given all the glory to Jesus Christ. I wish every little league and high school baseball player could know about the faith of Albert Pujols. All the kids that want to be like him need to know that he just wants to be like Jesus. Maybe you want to share this blog today with some coaches and young people in your area.

You may not hit 700 home runs, or win accolades in any sport, but you do have a platform. How you spend your life is your platform for either making money or making ministry. It's either bringing glory to you or bringing glory to God.

Jesus said, " Do not work for food that spoils, but for food that endures to eternal life, which the Son of Man will give you. For on him God the Father has placed his seal of approval." (John 6:27)

Who do you want to be like?

LIFE LESSON

THE OPPORTUNITY WORK OFFERS

A SOURCE OF EMPOWERMENT!

Willie Mays was born in Birmingham, Alabama, in a time when segregation was practiced throughout the United States. He was a great athlete, but his skin was the wrong color. For that reason, he didn't get as many opportunities early in his career.

Rickwood Field was home to the Birmingham Black Barons. It is the oldest professional baseball stadium in America! It came to life on Tuesday night, June 19, 2024, when it hosted the first National League baseball game played in Alabama. The purpose was to highlight the accomplishments of the Negro league players. Major league baseball stars attended to pay tribute to a lot of people who never received a lot of recognition.

Willie Mays went on to become a great player. He had enough talent and a lot of opportunities to be one of the first blacks to integrate into major league baseball. He was a star.

Rickwood Field gave Willie Mays an opportunity to play baseball. He never forgot it. He died at age 93 just two days before the great celebration at Rickwood. The big clock at Rickwood is always set to the time of 8:24. Those are the two numbers that Willie Mays wore in baseball -8 and 24.

Willie Mays described Rickwood Field as "a source of empowerment." He said that it was a place where he was given an opportunity. It was a platform that he and other Negro players could advance to bigger things. About one-half of the baseball Hall of Fame players played at Rickwood!

I love that phrase, "a source of empowerment." That's what we ought to call the church today. The church ought to be a place where anybody can come and discover how much God loves them, and the great gifts that God has given them, and give them a place to utilize those gifts. Rickwood did that for baseball players; the church ought to do it for everybody. Churches wouldn't be dying or declining if they were genuine sources of empowerment!

Rickwood was a place of opportunity. Willie Mays always said that if hadn't been for Rickwood, he would never have made it into the major leagues. How many young people today have the sense that their church is a source of empowerment-a place of giving them an opportunity? Young people seem to find their "empowerment" in other places- the church ought to be the place.

Rickwood was a place where you had to work hard in order to utilize your gifts. Church is not a place where we sit and soak, but it should be a place where we commit ourselves to serving and growing in utilizing our gifts through disciplined Bible study, prayer, service, and giving our faith away. Evaluate your church by asking if it's a place of empowerment where people can make commitments to see their gifts used by the Holy Spirit.

While Rickwood is the oldest baseball stadium in America, it has been improved many times. Everybody is impressed with the upgrades to Rickwood Field. This special television debut of the first national league baseball game played in Alabama required a lot of upgrading and change. If the church is going to be effective in today's world, it can't be like it was 100 or 10 or even one year ago. God wants to play His biggest game in churches-we need to be sure our churches are open to changes that can enlarge their empowerment possibilities!

Is your church a "source of empowerment?"

LIFE LESSON

AN OPPORTUNITY TO PERFORM

#18

The Boston Celtics set a new record for the most NBA championships. on June 18, 2024, when they beat the Dallas Mavericks to win number 18. That puts them one ahead of the Los Angeles Lakers. I was glad to see the Boston Celtics win for the following reasons:

1. Their coach Joe Mazzulla wore a unique black coaching shirt each game with a silver emblem on it. It was a cross. Every shirt he wore had a cross on it. When he was interviewed after the winning game, he didn't put on the NBA Championship t-shirt but put on one that said, "But first-let me thank God." He explained that his faith was the most important thing in his life. Everything else falls into place when faith is in first place-the right place. He is my kind of coach! (Read Matthew 6:33)

2. When the Celtic players were interviewed, each of them began with acknowledging the goodness of God. Their best player, Jason Tatum, was asked how he performed so well year after year. He said that God had given him the talent and a place to play where he could utilize his talent to the best of his ability. He thanked God for that. Other players interviewed first acknowledged God before answering questions. (Read Mtthew 10:32)

3. The Celtics play as a team. They have some great individual stars, but they pride themselves on teamwork. When they put all five players around the perimeter, and each one can shoot threes or

drive, they are considered to be "practically unstoppable." They usually make two or three extra passes in order to give a teammate a better shot to score. They put as much emphasis on the number of assists as they do points scored. (Read Matthew 5:41)

4. I heard about the Dallas Mavericks doing some trash talking before the Series. They publicly stated that Jaylen Brown was the Celtic's best player. That was intended to be an indication of how weak their team might be. Guess who the most valuable player in the Series was-Jaylen Brown! His teammates were going to be sure that he had a good series, and he exceeded their expectations. (Read Ecclesiastes 4:12)

5. The coach, Joe Mazzulla, and team members gave credit to the Celtics who had gone before them and won the 17 NBA Championships. They loved looking up at the ceiling and seeing all the championship banners and giving thanks to the people who made their opportunities possible. It's a great message to us in America during this 4th of July time when we need to be more mindful of what the people in the past have done for us and given us the freedoms that we enjoy. (Read Deuteronomy 6:10-12)

The Celtics were the sixth team to win the NBA Championship in the last six years a different team every year. If the Celtics continue to practice these kinds of fundamental principles, I predict that the streak of a different team winning every year will be broken next year!

The Celtics practice a lot of Biblical principles that are so applicable in the church, in business, and my personal life. Let's learn and live these lessons from the best basketball team in the world.

How is your team doing?

LIFE LESSON

HOW TO COACH

A REALLY BRIGHT STARR!

One small decision can change the course of your life. It happened in the life of Bart Starr.

In his sophomore year at Lanier High School, he went out for football, but didn't last but a couple of days. He quit the team. His father gave him a choice. He could either go back and play football or he could be in charge of the Starr's yard and garden. Bart liked football better than keeping a garden, so two weeks into his sophomore year he made the decision that changed his life. He went back to football.

He got some playing time at Lanier because the starting quarterback broke his leg. He spent a summer at the University of Kentucky where Bear Bryant was coaching. The great quarterback Babe Parilli worked with Bart Starr and helped him improve his passing game. Everybody thought he would go to Kentucky, but never underestimate the power of a girlfriend.

He had been introduced to Cherry Morton who was a student at Auburn. He decided to go to Alabama because it wasn't so far from Auburn. His dad really liked that decision. His record at Alabama was average because he played for a coach who didn't like to throw the ball.

When the pro draft came, Bart Starr was one of the last people selected I have been told that he was selected because an assistant coach at Auburn University had some friends in the front office of the Green Bay Packers. The Packers trusted the judgement of the Auburn coach when he insisted that they

34

take Bart Starr. At the end of the draft, they did. Think about that-an Auburn coach helped an Alabama player become a star in the pros!

Bart Starr played for Vince Lombardi who was a tough, detailed, no-nonsense kind of coach. He saw in Bart Starr what nobody else saw. He made him the starting quarterback. Green Bay won the first two Super Bowl games, and in both games, Bart Starr was the Most Valuable Player! From a decision to come back and play football as a sophomore at Lanier High School, to the best quarterback in professional football-that's Bart Starr!

His parents remained in Montgomery. They were strong Methodists. When I moved to Montgomery, they would very often come to church league softball games and basketball games. For most people, there is not anything less entertaining than church league sports. The Starrs loved it. There is a baseball complex in south Montgomery named The Ben Starr Park.

Bart and Dan Law called me one day a few years ago and said that we ought to have a function for one of the great running backs at Alabama, Bimbo Melton. He wasn't doing well physically. Bimbo was my first sports hero when I was in elementary school in Wetumpka. He married Susan Sewell, who was my neighbor. Susan's brother John and I would hide in the bushes and watch Bimbo kiss her good night. I felt really important working with Bart Starr for a function for Bimbo at Little Sam's Café in Wetumpka. Bart was always trying to help somebody who was down.

I learned a lesson from Bart. If people criticize you, take it as constructive criticism. God always sees you and me not as other people see us but as who He sees we could become. Always look at yourself the way God sees you. Always be interested in helping others. I was privileged to know one of the greatest football players and leaders ever to grow up in the State of Alabama, I thank God for that.

What is your life teaching?

LIFE LESSON

DECISIONS DETERMINE DESTINY

A REAL WINNER

One of the exciting, successful, young professional football players this year has been C.J. Stroud, a rookie quarterback for the Houston Texans He has had an incredible year. He led Houston to the playoffs for the first time since 2019. In the regular 2023 season, he passed for 4,108 yards, 29 touchdowns, and only 5 interceptions. He will probably be selected as the offensive rookie of the year.

He always gives the credit to God. After leading the Texans to a close win over Tampa Bay, he responded to a reporter's question with these words, "First and foremost, man, I gotta give all glory and praise to my Lord and Savior, Jesus Christ. I've been going through a lot, on and off the field, but when you give your life to the Lord, He gives you opportunities, and it's what you do with them."

Stroud's father was a pastor who made some bad decisions. He had to serve a long prison term in California while Stroud was in high school. He and his family encountered many financial hardships and housing insecurity.

During that time, Stroud's faith was tested and almost lost. He went with a fellow teammate at Ohio State to a worship service. Both came under deep conviction about what God wanted them to do with their lives. They made commitments to Christ and Stroud's life. turned around. He said, "It gave me a better feeling than winning a football game!"

Today, Stroud spends his time sharing the Good News. He quickly lets you know that he plays football to have a platform to spread the Good News of what Jesus Christ can do in your life.

When asked about how he has been able to navigate all his personal challenges, he always gives God the credit for helping him to be victorious. He says, "God has battle-tested me. I have the armor of God on me." He went on to say in one interview, "I am blessed enough to wake up every day and to walk, to talk, to smell, to interact with people, and to play football"

ESPN's Lisa Salters welcomed Stroud to the 2024 playoffs and asked how that sounded to him. He replied, "It's a blessing. I'm blessed to be the vessel that Christ picked to lead this great franchise, so I can do nothing but thank the Lord." He led Houston to victory in the first playoff game and set records for a rookie quarterback!

Success is not measured by who wins the most ballgames, but who wins in the most important game in town, which is life. C. J. Stroud has a huge future in professional football. He even has a bigger future in sharing how to really win in life through commitment to Jesus Christ. And, he has a huge, huge future knowing where he will spend eternity!

Football is C.J. Stroud's platform. What is yours? Do you see yourself as simply having a job, or a platform to carry out God's purpose? While professional football players get a lot of publicity, the Bible reminds us that each of us has a light to shine and we can be the salt of the earth. We are also reminded that when the smallest of all seeds, a mustard seed, is planted it grows into a huge tree.

How are you going to handle your adversities? When you accomplish something, do you take credit, or give the credit to God? Is your greatest motivation to succeed in order that you might reach more people with the Good News of God's grace?

C. J. Stroud is a winner! You can be a winner too!

LIFE LESSON

THE WIN THAT IS IMPORTANT

IRRELEVANT OR RELEVANT?

Brock Purdy was the last person chosen in the 2022 NFL draft. That person receives the title "Mr. Irrelevant." Nobody wanted him. The San Francisco 49ers took him.

He would be the least likely person to become a super star two years later in the NFL. Statistics were against him, but he never relied on statistics. In 2024, he ultimately relies on God's plan for his life, and he wants to be in the center of God's plan, He has quarterbacked the 49ers to the 58th Super Bowl. He has gone from Mr. Irrelevant to his new title of Mr. Elite Relevant! (I gave him that new title.)

He brought his team back from a 17-point deficit in the second half of the playoff win over the Detroit Lions. When reporters asked how he handled that, he said, "So when I'm down and at the half, honestly, I'm just thinking, 'all right God, you've taken me here, and win or lose, I'm going to glorify you. That's my peace, that's the joy, that's the steadfastness, that's where I get it from. And that's the honest truth."

In that remarkable playoff game against the Detroit Lions. He repeatedly did what experts said he couldn't do. He only averaged 2.4 yards a game running during the year. He ran the ball for 52 yards, with 33 coming after contact! All three of his scrambles were for first downs! He completed 13 of 16 passes for 174 yards, a touchdown, and a 132.8 quarterback rating! His combined yards passing and rushing were the most ever by a 49ers QB in a conference title game victory. Remember that Joe Montana and Steve Young were former 49er quarterbacks!

He went on to say that it was God who had taken him to where he is in life at this point, and he is going to trust Him for the future. When asked about a prediction in the Super Bowl, he said, "Win or lose I will give the glory to God."

Purdy looks like a college kid. He has a big smile on his face. The players believe in him. He has had a tremendous Christian impact on that team, and everybody associated with it.

He is a breath of fresh air for football fans. Many people don't recognize the air when it's fresh, but those who do take a deep breath and appreciate what his Christian witness means!

Football experts said that he doesn't have the physical and mental talents for a great quarterback, but that doesn't stop him. He just keeps playing, making unbelievable plays, and giving all the glory to God.

Maybe you are not the most talented or smartest person in your class or profession. You might even be one of those "last persons drafted." You can sit down and complain about what you don't have, or you can commit what you do have to God and let Him use you. It's your choice! Brock Purdy would say that you and God always make a majority!

Please don't read this and just sit and admire a football player. God can take you from Irrelevant to Relevant-maybe even Elite Relevant! Always remember to give God the glory.

Winning or losing a Super Bowl is not the most important thing in Purdy's life. His future won't depend on the outcome of that game. His future is bright in doing what God put him here to do-to be a good witness for Him and his future doesn't just include this life, but he knows where he will spend eternity. That's the most relevant future you can have!

Are you leaning towards being Irrelevant or Relevant? Would you let God make you Elite Relevant?

LIFE LESSON

LOOK WHAT GOD CAN DO

A WINNER'S WITNESS!

Women's college basketball reached new heights of popularity during the recent NCAA tournament. The final game had a TV viewing audience of 24 million, and an average of 18.7 million viewers. That is the most viewers ever to watch basketball at any level, according to Nielsen. It was the second most watched non-Olympic sporting event on US television since women's soccer beat Japan in 2019.

Coach Dawn Staley of the South Carolina Gamecocks played a big part in that growth in popularity. This was her third national championship in seven years. She has only lost one game in two years.

But I admire her, not only because of the accomplishments of her well-coached team, but because of her boldness in expressing her Christian faith. She prepares a devotional for her team members. They pray together and she shares her faith. She is very vocal in all of her Interviews about her strong faith. For her, winning girls to faith is as important as winning games for fans.

The Freedom From Religious Foundation has gone to court to try to stop her. In my eyes, that's a compliment to her faith! The issue was a statement she made on March 31, 2024. She was questioned about how she handled the one loss last year. She said, "I am a believer because God makes things come true. When you're at your worst, He's at His best."

The University of South Carolina president, Michael Amiridis, received a letter from FFRF alleging, "Since we first brought this issue to the University's attention, Coach Staley has only ramped up her use of religious rhetoric in official communications through her role as a university employee. She has also continued her practice of preparing gameday devotionals for players and sharing chosen Bible verses on her social media pages as Head Coach of South Carolina's Women's Basketball."

While I might not agree with Coach Staley on all issues, I applaud her on what's she's doing. I pray that God will increase her boldness, her witness, and raise up many more like her!

She is also a class lady. She is always complimentary of the opposing teams and their players. She doesn't try to take credit for all the big things she has done. While her team won the championship and were a huge part of the increase in TV viewers, she very humbly gave credit to a superstar, Caitlin Clark, as contributing the most. Coach Staley said that Clark had, "carried the biggest load in accordance with that success."

While we need more coaches like Dawn Staley, we also need more businesspeople, politicians, young people, moms and dads, and teachers we need more people like her in every section of society. Are you willing to be one of those? It's one thing to admire and praise her it's more important to do what she does!

Jesus said, "Everyone who confesses Me before men, I will confess him before my Father" (Matthew 10:32) He also said, "When I am lifted up, I will draw all people to my Father" (John 12:32)

A Christian coach is telling the world about her faith, and refusing to bow to pressure from those who would oppose her expression of her Christian faith. Thank you, Lord!

What is your witness?

LIFE LESSON

THE POWER OF A WITNESS

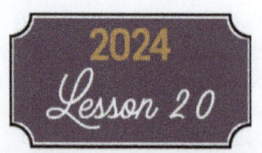

COACHES, REFEREES, AND PEOPLE

For several years I had the opportunity to speak at the Fellowship of Christian Athletes Coaches' Family Conference I get to deliver six messages a conference to college and high school coaches. Coach Jimmy Reeves and his wife Lisa run this conference.

They bring in some outstanding people who give a witness at one of the services. This year one witness was given by Ronnie Baynes. He was the high school coach who won state championships in baseball then started refereeing football. He went from college to the NFL where he spent fourteen years on the field as an NFL official, then another twelve years in the NFL home office overseeing officials.

Not all coaches have a great appreciation for referees. Ronnie Baynes reminded them that he was also once a coach. He had a strong witness to those coaches.

He told some interesting stories about officiating in the Super Bowl and NFL playoff games. He admitted that officials are human, and make mistakes, but he also reminded the coaches that sometimes they make coaching mistakes and occasionally they have a player who will make a mistake.

Making mistakes in life is a part of life. The important thing is that we confess our mistakes, ask for forgiveness, and try to become better at what we do and make less mistakes.

I am very proud that both Auburn and Alabama basketball teams have been to the Final Four. I remember watching the game when Auburn was playing Virginia in the semi-finals and had a small lead in the last minute of the game. A Virginia guard lost control of the ball in the back court and retrieved it and started dribbling it again. They scored a basket which ultimately led to Auburn's defeat. Most everybody in the stands saw that the Virginia guard double dribbled the ball. It was quite obvious, but was not changed. Officials do make mistakes.

When I finished Seminary, I decided to referee high school basketball. I got my referee's shirt and official patch. My first game was against Beulah and Beauregard who at that time only played basketball, but they played it thirteen months a year! They were bitter rivals. There were so many people at that game that folks were literally sitting on parts of the court. I was from Opelika, a few miles away, and most of the fans knew me. Every time I blew the whistle, half the fans didn't like it. I actually refereed two basketball games-my first and my last!

As long as humans participate in sports, there will be mistakes on the part of the referees and the players and the coaches. As long as people are people, we will make mistakes. The Bible is clear that we "all sin and fall short of God's glory." (Romans 3:23) The Bible is also clear that, "If we confess our sins, He is faithful to forgive our sins and to cleanse us from all wickedness." (1 John 1:9) The good thing about the Christian faith is that we are not perfect, just forgiven. Because we are forgiven by God, we need to forgive other people.

When you attend sporting events, please don't yell at the referees and criticize them. Video replays have shown that most of the time they are right.

Remember, there is one Major Referee who will someday at our death, make the most important call that will last for eternity-He won't make a mistake and there will be no instant replay. Your decisions in this life will make His decision easy.

Be sure His final whistle signals a touchdown and not a penalty!

LIFE LESSON

RESPECT THE REFEREES

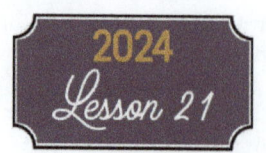

RECORDS-BASEBALL AND LIFE

What do the records show? It really depends on how the records were compiled.

In the 1930s and '40s, baseball was racially segregated. You had the Negro League statistics, as well as the Major League Baseball records which only contained white players.

It raises the question of who had the most hits, the most home runs the most strike outs, etc. In the last three years a 17-member panel has been vetting thousands of Negro League box scores to compile the new data for the official record books. Some of the great players like Satchel Paige, Buck Leonard, Cool Papa Bell, and Josh Gibson were excluded from the official records.

Seventy-seven years after the death of Josh Gibson, the slugging catcher, has become baseball's all-time batting champion! Major League Baseball decided it needed to correct what it called a "longtime oversight." Gibson had a lifetime average of .372 while playing for the Homestead Grays, along with some other teams. That placed him ahead of Ty Cobbs .367 lifetime average.

People discuss how well Gibson and others would have fared had baseball not been segregated. Some people are arguing that the Negra League seasons were much shorter, and the competition was not at the same level. Gibson had only 838 verified lifetime hits and Ty Cobb had 4,191. Gibson is credited for having the highest season batting average of 466, but only had 157 at-bats in 1945. They are not putting asterisks by anyone's name-just combining the statistics of both leagues into one record category.

I remember hearing that liars can figure, and figures can lie. It's really hard to compare apples to apples. Kevin Blackstone contends that "the Negro Leagues were never less than major, and the white-only major leagues were not as major as we've mythologized them to be."

It won't go in the record books, but the oldest living active baseball player today is Bill Gleason who is 99 years old. He threw out the first pitch for the celebration of Negro baseball games at Rickwood Field June 20, 2024. I called him "active" because he is now a preacher at Bethel Baptist Church and preaches every Sunday! Only a preacher could throw a strike at 99 years old!

I guess the discussion will go on about who holds the greatest records in baseball. What if we were as interested in measuring how well we serve in God's Kingdom and what would be the score if we determine how effectively we are using our gifts? We could do a lot of arguing about that, but the final authority for any records of the Christian faith rest solely with God. His records are not debatable, and you are measured not by who will receive the greatest honors, but who gave the most to God's Kingdom.

His records are not based on how much we get, but how much we give. His records are not based on how many homeruns we have, but on how many people we have helped come home. His records are not about how many strike outs we have, but how many bases we have helped people advance.

The most important score card reveals whether or not we struck out in following Him, how many people we carry home with us for eternity are we winning or losing?

What is your record?

LIFE LESSON

BREAKING RECORDS

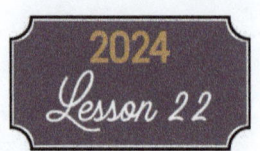

STRIIIIKE!!!

Cooper Murray is an 11-year-old Downs Syndrome boy. He was born in China and was found abandoned on a street corner when he was six months old. He lived the first four years of his life in an orphanage, 2016 changed his life when he was adopted by an American family. It opened the door for a new future for him and he is walking through it.

Cooper Murray loves baseball. He set a goal to throw out the first pitch at every major league baseball stadium in America. Already, six different teams have invited him to do that. The Chicago Cubs gave him the first chance and then the Boston Red Sox followed. I predict that he will be invited to all 30 major league ballparks.

He is really cute when he wears the uniform of the home team. He wears his cap backwards like the big ball players do. He wears a red cape. He shortens the distance to home plate. He checks the runner at 2nd base, kicks his leg high, and throws a strike.

The person catching the ball varies on each of the ball clubs. When he threw the first pitch at the Atlanta Braves game, the mascot received it He ran out to the mound and gave a high five to Cooper and a big hug The fans gave a standing ovation. One reporter said, "He knocked the fans' hearts out of the park."

They call him Coop. He is incredibly cute when he is interviewed. He has a great personality. He is the MVP at every gathering!

The reason he is doing this is not only because he loves baseball, but he and his family want to raise awareness of the opportunity to adopt kids with Downs Syndrome. They refer to the kids as kids with "special abilities." They are raising money to help pay the initial cost for a family to adopt.

Too often in life people who are blessed with good health take that health for granted and focus so much on things that are selfish. So many people want to take care of themselves. We see needs around us, but we don't extend ourselves to meet those needs.

Here is an 11-year-old Downs Syndrome boy who is making a difference in the lives of a lot of people. First there are thousands of baseball fans who would love to see him throw out the first pitch (it's also a good promotion for selling tickets).

He is also raising money that will make a difference in the lives of other Downs Syndrome kids. He has found a niche where he can make a difference, and he is really enjoying it.

Jesus said he didn't come into the world to be served but to serve and to give His life as a ransom for many. (Matthew 20:28) Servant leaders are what our nation needs to produce. Teaching kids and adults that it is more blessed to give than to receive is a much-needed lesson to learn.

The Murrays emphasize that every person has a song that we are meant to sing, and everybody has divine potential. What Cooper is doing helps "give voice to the voiceless children in foster homes and institutions in international countries." It's helping kids who are caught in tough circumstances.

What are you doing to make a difference?

LIFE LESSON

OVERCOMING OBSTACLES

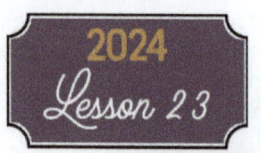

OPENING AND CLOSING OLYMPIC CEREMONIES

The opening ceremonies for the 2024 Olympics in Paris have become the most controversial in the history of the Olympics. Much of the pageantry was, in my opinion, despicable and out of touch with respect for basic religious beliefs. I realize both sides have explanations for what happened. I am including parts of a blog about the opening and closing ceremonies that I wrote following the 2020 Olympics which I want to remember as the purpose of the opening and closing ceremonies.

The purpose of the opening ceremony is to allow the athletes of each nation to stand with their nation's flag. The closing ceremony in 2020 did not have the athletes standing with their own flag, but represented the Olympic games as being people from different nations walking together. That's the real meaning of the Olympics.

This tradition started in 1956 at the Melbourne Games. You might remember that high political tensions had caused several countries not to participate. Those games became famous when the water polo match between Hungary and the Soviet Union ended in a bloody fight. The contest had to be cancelled when the violence broke out.

A 17-year-old Australian of Chinese descent suggested in an anonymous letter that those games should end with people walking together as "only one nation." The letter was sent to Kent Hughes, the chairman of the Melbourne Organizers' Committee. He liked the idea, so the closing ceremony took place with people coming in together.

It wasn't until 1986 that the writer of that letter was revealed as John Wing. When questioned about it, he said that he wanted history to show that the Olympics could go from "bloody" to the "friendly games."

Our world today needs to go from competition that is producing bloodshed to community that can produce peace and harmony! We need less walking behind the flags of our own thoughts and positions and more walking with other people. We must learn to live together!

The word community is composed of two words-common and unity. Common refers to the fact that everybody is included. Unity refers to togetherness, teamwork, and solidarity, and that leads people to live in peace, civility, and love.

We have enough competition in the world we need community. The One who can give community is God's son, Jesus Christ. He died to bring all people into a new relationship to God so that all people could live together meaningfully. Jesus said, "God so loved the world..." (John 3:16) The word "world" includes everybody. Only God can create a community in which people can live in peace!

Religious denominations need to quit competing and start cooperating in creating God's community. Cities need to quit competing and focus on how we can improve all human relationships. Nations and races need to quit competing and discover the power of genuine Christian relationships. We need less opening ceremonies and more closing ceremonies!

An Australian of Chinese descent, John Wing, had a great idea for the Olympics. A Jewish Carpenter had a greater idea for changing the understanding of relationships. (Matthew 22:37-40) Our world needs community. Our world needs to experience peace, respect, and love.

What opening or closing ceremony does your life project?

LIFE LESSON

OLYMPIAN COMMUNICATION

WATCH YOUR STEP!

Exercise is very important. Walking is one of the best ways to exercise We set goals as to how many steps we should take each day. Those steps are usually counted by a watch, a pedometer or even a cell phone. I just checked my phone, and yesterday I walked 7,279 steps.

There are some insurance companies who give reductions to participants who regularly record their steps and meet a specified goal. There are also groups of people who have contests to see who can walk the most steps in a week or a month. My great friend, Rev. David Bush, serves in Arkansas. I've been with him several times at his church in Stuttgart, and at his present assignment in El Dorado.

A few years ago, I, along with a couple of friends, George Dunklin and Allen Homra, encouraged David to start walking more. Sometimes there is a fine line between encouraging and pestering. At any rate -the goal was to see him walk. We succeeded! He has become very disciplined in his walking. He has even won several contests for the most steps taken! He's encouraging us now!

I had the privilege of going to the first meeting in Montgomery several years ago called by Judge Joe Phelps. He had a vision of a program called STEP (Strategies To Elevate People). Churches united and started taking some important steps to making a difference in people's lives. STEP, under the leadership of Cedric Fluker, is still a strong ministry in the River Region. STEP ministry can occur in any region in the world!

While the quantity of our steps is important, we also need to look at the quality of our steps. Where do our steps lead us? Are we walking in the purpose that God has for us? We need to walk "In His steps." (1 Peter 2:21)

Just before Palm Sunday, Jesus was walking with His disciples and came to a fork in the road. He could either take steps towards Jerusalem where He knew those would be His final steps, or He could take the other road and avoid what would happen during Holy Week. The Bible says, "He set His face steadfast to go to Jerusalem." (Luke 9:51) He knew which steps He needed to take.

On Good Friday He endured ridicule, physical abuse, and flogging. He then started taking some steps toward Golgotha. Those are the most important steps in history! They took Him to the very place that fulfilled His purpose in dying for you and me. Those steps also made possible the resurrection on Easter.

Where are your steps taking you? Some people take wrong steps that get them in with the wrong crowd, and that gets them into trouble. Other people prayerfully ask God to direct their steps so that they lead to the right crowd and the right place. "We can make our plans, but the Lord determines our steps." (Proverbs 16:9) Life takes on a new dimension when we make every step count to serve Him and fulfill His purpose for us.

STEP DOWN from a prideful attitude.

STEP UP to the challenge God puts before you.

STEP IN to God's power and purpose.

STEP OUT to the high calling that God has for you.

STEP OVER the obstacle Satan puts in front of you.

STEP UNDER somebody's load and help carry it.

LIFE LESSON

WALK IN HIS STEPS

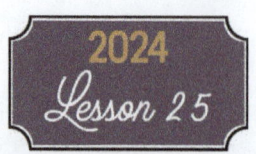

REVIVE US AGAIN!

Auburn University is experiencing revival! On September 12, 2023, about 5,000 students gathered in the basketball arena at Auburn for a worship service focusing on "Auburn United." The spirit of God started to move in that worship experience, and it didn't end when the closing prayer was given!

One student wanted to be baptized so a lot of the crowd heard about that and made an unplanned trip to a nearby lake. WSFA reported that about 200 students were baptized.

It's a powerful scene to see a couple of thousand college students standing around the lake and praying and singing. As each newly baptized person came out of the water, the cheer is reported to have compared with anything that was ever heard in Jordan-Hare Stadium or Neville Arena!

A beautiful picture of one of the men participating in the baptizing was head football coach, Hugh Freeze. He was experiencing the most important victory he will ever see at Auburn!

Coach Freeze was not the only coach there. Head basketball coach, Bruce Pearl, and head baseball coach, Butch Thompson, had promoted it and participated. Some of their players were baptized.

I've heard that it all started when one college girl started going to the basketball arena and praying for revival. Get that one girl, along with God, started this whole thing. A coach's wife joined in praying along with four other college girls. You now have five college students and an interested adult praying. They started a Bible study. It wasn't long before the group had grown to about 200 girls.

The group felt led to pray for some larger event. That's when the vision of a worship service came to reality. Actually, the worship service hasn't ended- it's continuing throughout that campus!

Dylan Cardwell is a big-name basketball recruit that God led to Auburn. When Coach Pearl took the basketball team to Israel this past spring. Dylan helped in baptizing several of the basketball players. Dylan teaches a weekly Bible Study and speaks to a lot of groups. I have heard him say, "I don't know what is going to happen next at Auburn, but God is clearly moving."

His vision is becoming a reality. The campus is on fire through the movement of God's Holy Spirit. Because it's a Godly fire, there will be a lot of people coming in with fire extinguishers trying to put it out. You will even have experienced firefighters trying to put out this fire. But this fire will not be put out!

There are other college campuses that I personally know where revival is taking place. Asbury College in Kentucky is in the midst of a great revival. Here in Montgomery, Dr. Mitchell Henry, President of Faulkner University, told me that 37 football players had been baptized in the last six weeks. I was in a worship service this summer where many of the women's soccer team at Samford University were baptized. And there are many others.

As our nation was being formed, 108 colleges were established, and 106 of those were Christian! That has drastically changed today. Let's go back to that early statistic!

What's happening right now at these colleges I've mentioned can happen at any college and any church. Pray and participate with students and God as we fan the flames of revival everywhere!

It's revival time!

LIFE LESSON

REVIVAL IS HAPPENING

IT'S PRIME TIME!

Deion Sanders has dominated the news about college football this year. An article in U.S. Today suggested that he could be the most famous college football coach in history! Prime time has a new meaning, and it doesn't refer to television.

In the past thirty years, Deion has made multiple commercials for outstanding products. His AFLAC commercials with Nick Saban are some of the most popular today. He has hosted a Miss USA pageant He played both professional baseball and professional football. In five days in 1989, he had two doubles and a homerun for the Yankees, then flew to Atlanta to score a touchdown to beat the Rams!

He was hired this year as the University of Colorado head football coach. His popularity escalated as Colorado played their archrival Colorado State. The televised game did not even start until 10:00 pm on the East Coast. That's not television prime time, but Coach "Prime Time" led his team to a double overtime win and 11.1 million television viewers saw it! Wow! That's six times as many viewers as watched the highly advertised Alabama/Texas football game a week earlier!

I love his outspoken witness to his Christian faith. He has an Instagram post captioned "Jesus." He said, "Sex won't satisfy you. Fame won't satisfy you. Drugs won't satisfy you. Money won't satisfy you. Alcohol won't satisfy you.

Success won't satisfy you. Life is empty without Jesus. He is the only one who can satisfy your heart."

When he was introduced at Colorado as the head coach, he thanked Colorado for selecting him, but he felt it was really God who chose him for that position. He said, "Out of all the persons in the world, God chose me. For that, I thank Him and you."

He has had some big physical, spiritual, and emotional challenges in his life. He is realistic that life has mountaintops and valleys. He was quoted when he prayed, "Lord, I thank you for yesterday because if it weren't for yesterday, I wouldn't be prepared for today. I am appreciative of the ups, downs, comings, goings, the light, the darkness, the good and the bad. I thank you for it all."

He got his nickname when he was playing high school basketball and scored 35 points to beat a big rival. The newspaper headlines called him "Prime Time"-and it has stuck. Today, it is often shortened to "Prime."

He gives credit to coaches, but he always remembers the "little people." Look at his shirt that he wears on the sideline each week when he coaches. On the right sleeve, you will see JC. That stands for Jimmie Callahan who was the equipment manager at Florida State. Deion remembers him every time he coaches because he had such a big influence on him in college. How many people reading this article know the names of the "little people" in your organization?

I don't know how many more games Deion will win this year, but watch out for the future. The most important wins he has are not on the football field but in the lives of students, players, and adults throughout America. Pray for him-and all coaches.

Isn't this a prime time for you to make a difference?

LIFE LESSON

WHAT'S REALLY IMPORTANT

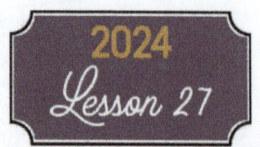

PUT ME IN COACH!

I love coaches and appreciate what they do. An important part of my ministry now deals with coaches and athletic teams. I believe that coaches have a great opportunity to be used by God to change the lives of young people. Someone once said, "If any adult can get a foot in the door with today's youth, that foot will be wearing shoes with cleats on them."

Joe Kennedy was the coach at Bremerton High School in Washington. He prayed with his team in the locker room and on the field after each game. His school administration told him to stop. Through a series of legal proceedings, he was suspended and lost his job for praying. But that didn't stop him he said he was going to continue praying.

Eight years later on September 1, 2023, the Supreme Court of the United States ruled that he was denied his rights and could follow guidelines to pray with his athletes. Praise God! Pray for coaches to have more boldness in reaching young people.

In the 1980s, Charles Lee was head coach of the Jeff Davis Volunteers, which was one of the largest high schools in Alabama. Coach Lee's young assistant coach, Bobby Eskew, had a stroke following a game and died a few days later. Coach Lee asked me to come and speak to the team. I did and continued going every week and speaking to the team for that year and the next eleven years!

Most of that coaching staff joined the church at Frazer and became active. Head Coach Lee and defensive coach coordinator, Bubba Lewis, gave me complete freedom in relating to those young athletes. The coaches sometimes complained that I made too many suggestions to them for coaching. They reminded me that they didn't preach on Sunday. I reminded them that my suggestions for creative plays to run and defensive schemes led them to a couple of state championships!

I have had the opportunity to speak at team chapels and FCA huddle groups at the University of Alabama, Auburn, Troy, Alabama State, Clemson, Huntingdon College, and several others. I have spoken at most of the high schools in the River Region.

All of these opportunities to speak to players and coaches have been in athletic facilities or on the playing field. I must confess that I was never confronted about the fact that I could be doing something "illegal." I am thankful for a coach like Joe Kennedy who was willing to stand up and make a difference. We need more coaches and American citizens like him!

Coaches have had a huge influence on my life. My high school coach in Opelika was Sam Mason, and in that day, he coached football, basketball, baseball and drove the bus! My Young Harris Junior College basketball coach was Luke Rushton. My Huntingdon basketball coach was Neal Posey. I want to share with you about their influence on me in a future opportunity.

I have been blessed by coaches. That's why I am grateful to be invited to speak at several different coach's conferences. Just this week, I had an email from a head coach with a major division-one school thanking me for the influence I have had on him, his staff, and players. My daily podcasts and radio messages, weekly blog, and daily videos have enabled me to give back some of the things I received from coaches.

Pray for coaches. Encourage coaches. Thank coaches for their influence on your community. Support coaches when they are bold in expressing their convictions.

Thanks coach!

LIFE LESSON

COACHES THAT REALLY KNOW COACHING

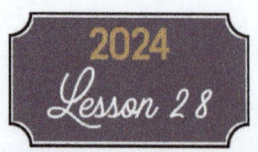

FELLOWSHIP OF CHRISTIAN ATHLETES

The Fellowship of Christian Athletes is one of the greatest organizations in our country. Please don't ever hesitate to generously offer financial support to the organization that is changing the population of Heaven! One of my great privileges was to serve for eight years on the National Board of Directors of the Fellowship of Christian Athletes.

Mark Jackson was a Frazer member and an FCA staff member. I invited Mark to give a witness at Frazer. I will never forget his bringing a huge box to the pulpit and dumping hundreds and hundreds of cards on the pulpit. He then told the congregation that each of these cards represented a student in Central Alabama who had accepted Christ through FCA. That service was on both local and national television.

Frazer's commitment also involved financial support. John Gibbons is a great leader. He has been the State of Alabama Director of FCA for several years. He said that Frazer gave more money to FCA in one year than any church has ever given in a year! What an investment!

Today, in Alabama, there are 832 FCA campus ministries ministering to athletes. There are 92 staff members. There are over 75,000 participating athletes and coaches in the FCA ministry weekly or monthly. This year there have been over 3,000 first-time faith commitments!

Wow! There are many other aspects of the ministry in Alabama, such as, five marriage enrichment retreats for coaches and their spouses.

One young man, Tyrone Peterson, received a Frazer scholarship to go to a national FCA camp at Black Mountain North Carolina. He had become a serious problem child, as he was placed in several different foster homes and Brantwood Children's Home.

Jesus changed his life at that conference. He went from being the guy that nobody wanted to be around to one of the most popular high school boys in the City of Montgomery! I loved walking with him in the Eastdale Mall and most every student of any race or school spoke to him.

He went to Troy University and now is a teacher and coach here in Montgomery. He has a marvelous wife and two beautiful girls. Montgomery is different because of Tyrone Peterson, and Tyrone is different because of Jesus Christ and FCA!

It was a great privilege for him to stay in our home during holiday seasons. I've always had a morning devotional on the radio on WLWI at 6:00 A.M. Tyrone got all the kids at Brantwood up every morning and had them in the gathering room by 5:50 A.M. to listen to the devotion. He then led them in prayer.

I wrote a book last year called "Life Lessons Learned from Sports." There are fifty-four lessons involving coaches and athletes. You can order the book from our ministry for $10.00 plus $5.00 postage. Many leaders and churches in different communities have given a copy to each coach in their school system. Many parents and grandparents have used it to teach lessons to their kids. I am working on another book I hope to bring out next year on more life lessons in sports.

Please pray for God to raise up more Godly coaches, change the lives of more athletes, and raise up more organizations like FCA that has a ministry to all students!

LIFE LESSON

A DIFFERENCE - MAKING MINISTRY

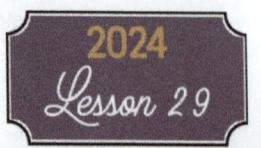

BE PREPARED

When preparation is adequate, performance becomes productive and exciting. Preparation that is overlooked or sloppily done causes disappointment and failure. Preparation is the key.

I always admired Roger Staubach as a college and professional football player. He was a winner on the field, but he was a bigger winner in how he lived his life. I have become more interested in his career at the Naval Academy since we have a grandson, David Hixon, who is attending there and the starter on the football team.

Roger Staubach was a multiple year all pro. He was All American in college. His performance was always excellent. He paid meticulous attention to details, was extremely disciplined, and knew how to prioritize his time, effort, energy, and spiritual growth. He said much of his life's success was summed up when he was quoted one day as saying, "The sensational accomplishments in life are the result of unsensational preparation."

We like the accomplishments-but it's hard to do the things that get us ready for those accomplishments. The sensational accomplishments must always be preceded by the unsensational hard work to prepare for that moment.

I know that all people have different talents and for some of us it takes more preparation. Sensational accomplishments are relative, but I think that whatever our skill and intelligence level is, we each will be held accountable for how we apply the skills and talents that we have. Proper preparation will always be a strong contributing factor to how much we can accomplish.

I remember in college I had a couple of professors who would give "pop tests." We would come to class, and nobody had any idea that we would have a test, which you had better be prepared for. The fact that you didn't know when the pop test would occur indicated that you had better be prepared every day that you go to class. I got an "A" in that class because I was always prepared for the "pop test"

In life, we don't know when the big tests will sometimes come. They will come. We might have some warning signs that the big test is coming, but it can come unexpectedly. The important thing is to be prepared for whatever comes.

We usually know about hurricanes and tornadoes before they become reality. There is time for preparation. Some people prepare some people don't.

Automobile accidents and unexpected tragedies don't announce in advance that they are coming. They just come. Some people are prepared, and some people are not. "Be prepared, and prepare yourself, you and all that are assembled about you." (Ezekial 28:7)

I had a funeral recently and someone asked me if the man died suddenly. I responded that he did die suddenly. Everybody dies suddenly. You are here one second in this world, and the next second you have left this world and entered eternity. What happens then is whether or not you are prepared for death and eternity. Some people are prepared-others are not.

The possibilities of performance are preceded by proper preparation.

LIFE LESSON

ARE YOU PREPARING PROPERLY?

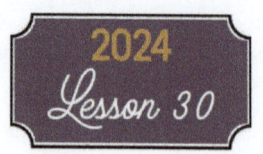

A GOLFER'S SERMON

One of the upcoming professional golfers is Harry Higgs. He recently won two tournaments in a row on the Korn Ferry Tour.

He was victorious in a playoff at the Knoxville Open on May 27, 2024. He received the trophy and had an opportunity to speak. Remember that the Korn Ferry Tour is just under the PGA Tour and all the players are looking for victories and enough points to get a card to play on the PG Tour. The Knoxville Open was a big step for Harry Higgs.

He confessed that his brief speech would be out of the norm. He apologized if people were expecting something else, but he had something he wanted to say-wanted everybody to hear it.

He began by honoring Grayson Murray. Grayson was thirty years old and played on the PGA Tour. He had actually won a couple of PGA Tournaments. He was playing in the Charles Swabb Challenge and finished the first two rounds. He then dropped out on Friday, May 25, citing the fact that he had an illness. He caught a plane back to Florida. The golf world learned on Saturday that he had died. His parents reported he had taken his own life on Saturday.

Higgs knew Murray well. After acknowledging Murray, Higgs said he would like to say some things not just to the golf world, but to every person.

Higgs said, "We lost yesterday morning one of our own, somebody who went through a lot of difficult things. Somebody who was open and honest about it. I thought about this moment and how I could remember Grayson. This golf stuff and the result is lovely sure, but it's just not that meaningful."

"One thing that I thought of last night when I was lying in bed, is I am telling everybody here-and I'm going to do this myself as well-each day say something nice to the ones you love and also make it a point to say something nice to somebody you do not even know."

"The world is a difficult place and getting more difficult. I have been blessed with great parents and a great support system. I haven't had serious battles mentally. The Lord knows how many people do have them and it's only ever increasing."

"Everybody here could be a difference-the difference. Lighten up somebody's day, it could mean the world to them."

Higgs' victory speech was one of the better sermons preached on that Sunday. Each of us encounters people who are struggling. Everybody needs a kind, encouraging word. None of us ever knows what lies around the next corner for us or for others.

If you are struggling today, God can meet you where you are and give you what you need to win that battle, which is more important than winning any golf tournament. I hope you surround yourself with people who encourage you and are honest with you in helping you. We need each other.

The answer to all issues in life is found in a relationship to God through His Son, Jesus Christ. If you are not sure of that relationship, please talk with a Christ follower who can help you experience the victory of making that decision.

I don't play golf, but I really liked Harry Higgs' sermon. I plan to practice it. Will you join me?

LIFE LESSON

AN UNEXPECTED SERMON

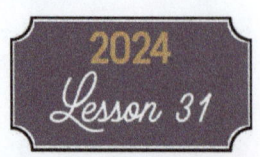

GOD GUARANTEES HIS PICKS

I was in the sixth grade at Hohenberg Elementary School in Wetumpka Alabama. I was watching a group of the older guys pick teams for a pick-up game of basketball. A life-changing event occurred for me when one of the better players, Walter Albritton, picked me to play on his team. I had never been picked by the older guys before.

That small thing was big for me! Basketball became very important. It started me on a path to make All-State in the 10th grade, get a four-year college basketball scholarship, and be selected for a National All-Star team to play against Olympic teams from Asia and give a Christian witness.

Being picked for a team is very important. That's what Paul writes to the Ephesians about. It's one of the three letters that he wrote from prison, The purpose of the early chapters of this letter is to show how God has picked them for His team. The later chapters are about how the team will function.

The first big question was whether the Gentiles would be picked. In Ephesians 1:13, he makes it clear that Gentiles who have believed in Christ are picked. He identified them as His own by giving the Gentiles the Holy Spirit whom He had promised long ago. He then declares that the giving of the Holy Spirit is God's guarantee that the Gentiles have been picked.

Picked and guaranteed that's God's sign that the Gentiles and Jews are on God's team. When you believe in Christ and follow Him, you have been picked by Him because He gives the Holy Spirit to His people. The ministry of the Holy Spirit is to continue the work of Christ in the world and to offer His power so that all people might follow Him.

God's guarantee is always good. When you receive His guarantee the gift of the Holy Spirit-certain things become evident in your life. How would you answer these questions?

1. Have I received Christ and decided to follow Him?

2. Am I identified as a team member because of God's gift of His Holy Spirit?

3. Does the power of the Holy Spirit flow into and through my life?

4. Do I get frustrated and fail because I try to do things my own way?

5. Is the power of the Holy Spirit in my life evident because I praise and glorify Him? (Ephesians 1:14)

6. Do I share God's guarantee with others?

If you are a Gentile or Jew, male or female, slave or free-and your faith is in Jesus Christ (Galatians 3:26-29), God has identified you and picked you for His team, and receiving the gift of the Holy Spirit is God's guarantee of your selection. This is the greatest team on which you could ever play!

It's interesting to me to read how some professional athletes sign a huge contract worth a lot of dollars-but only a certain portion is guaranteed. God's guarantee to is

His team is 100% guaranteed!

God's guarantee is always good. Sometimes people have to go to court to determine whether a guarantee was really a valid guarantee. You never have to go to court to test God's guarantee because He gives us the Holy Spirit!

You've been picked! Are you ready to play?

LIFE LESSON

THE POWER OF A PICK

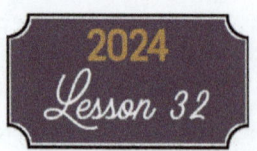

MARCH MADNESS OR MARCH GLADNESS

March Madness is a time when people like to predict winners of basket. ball games. Millions of people fill out March Madness brackets to show their skills.

I once thought Warren Buffett was growing senile when he offered to give $1 billion to anybody who had a perfect bracket. I learned that the odds of a perfect bracket are 1 in 92 quintillion-that's seventeen zeroes. You have a better chance of winning two consecutive lotteries than you do in completing a perfect March Madness bracket!

This year really proves the point of how bad we are at predicting. In the first round a 16th seed upset a number one seed-that's only the second time that's happened in the history of the NCAA Tournament. This year was unique because no number one seed was in the final four. In fact, there were three teams in the final four who had never been there before!

We think that recruiting McDonald's All-Americans should ensure wins. Not so. For the first time since 1979, this year's final four did not have a single high school McDonald's All-American playing!

This year's March Madness just indicates that there is no way to have confidence in predicting basketball outcomes. Filling out the brackets this year was just an exercise in futility.

It's sad how many people in life are always trying to predict and figure out how things are going to be. Life is more fickle than March Madness. Thinking that you've got everything figured out will turn out to be a bust. The Bible reminds us that there is a way that seems right to man, but the end of which is destruction. (Proverbs 14:12)

Holy Week is about events and principles you can count on. You will die. You will have no control over what happens after death unless you have accepted Jesus Christ as Savior and Lord. You cannot earn your way into Heaven. It is by grace and grace alone that you are saved. (Ephesians 2:4-10)

Making elaborate funeral plans won't help. I am one hundred percent sure that if you have been saved by faith, you will live forever with God. Jesus said, "If you have known me then you have known my Father." (John 14:5-7) We know the Father because we know His Son.

Paul assured us that because Christ rose from the dead, all who believe in Christ will rise again. No doubt! (I Corinthians 15:51-58) We also know that the Holy Spirit can fill our lives and give us power and direction to fulfill God's plan. (Acts 1:8)

You will never have a perfect bracket in March Madness-you are not that smart. You can be assured that what happened Holy Week will continue to be true today and forever. Trusting in Jesus alone for life abundant here and life eternal is never a gamble-because gambling involves a degree of chance. No chance that God and His Word are wrong!

March Madness is filling out brackets and watching basketball. March Sadness is seeing brackets busted. March Gladness is understanding Holy Week and knowing who is going to win in the most important game-the game of life.

Is your March Madness, or Sadness, or Gladness?

LIFE LESSON

WHAT'S YOUR PICK?

TWO LADIES - TWO LEGACIES

When you die, how will you be remembered? How long will you be remembered? What are the things for which you will be remembered? We refer to it as a legacy.

Two ladies died 26 days apart. They were at different ends of the age spectrum-80 and 18. They lived at different sections of our Nation Springfield, Ohio and Brantley, Alabama. They will be remembered for vastly different things. They each left a legacy.

Kathleen Dehmlow was 80 years old and died on May 31, 2018 in Springfield, Minnesota. Her obituary was brief. It said, "She abandoned her children, Gina and Jay, who were then raised by her parents. She will now face judgment. She will not be missed by Gina and Jay, and they understand that this world is a better place without her!"

Kathleen was born on the same day I was born-March 19, 1938. The newspaper that published her obituary, the Redwood Falls Gazette, verified that it was accurate, but decided to take it down a week later. What a terrible legacy to leave. 80 years old-that's how she will be remembered.

A beautiful young lady died Monday, June 25, 2018 in Brantley, Alabama. Alex Wilcox was 18 years old. She was the face of Brantley softball. She led

Brantley to four state championships over the last five years. Following her senior year she received a scholarship to play at Mississippi State.

The doctors discovered a reoccurrence of ovarian cancer in Alex. She only played 15 games at Mississippi State. She made a tremendous impact on people in Brantley and in Mississippi. The Mississippi State softball team wore special jerseys this year to honor her influence -even though it was over a brief time. Brantley's softball team wore a sticker on their helmets and a fake tattoo on their wrists to honor her.

I met her coach, Cindy Hawthorne, five years ago at a Fellowship of Christian Athletes family coach's conference. I've spoken at that conference every year since then. Cindy and other coaches from Brantley are always there. Cindy gives a strong witness about Alex's faith and inspiration.

Coach Hawthorne said, "We know where she is, and I just thank God for that assurance. I'm going to be with her again one day. No doubt about where she is spending eternity." Coach Hawthorne went on to say, "Her legacy will live on until the end of time." Her principal, Kris Odom said, "She left a legacy that will be here forever." "Until the end of time" and "forever" defines the length of Alex's legacy.

Her team won another state championship a few weeks ago at Lagoon Park here in Montgomery. Alex was able to attend the final game. The team requested that Alex come out and help receive the trophy. AHSAA Associate Director Tony Stallworth agreed. Alex didn't really want the recognition, but all of her friends, coaches and family insisted. She carried the trophy out to the pitcher's mound. In Brantley there is a street called Championship Drive that leads from Main Street to the softball complex. Alex's picture and the state championship banners. represent her legacy.

Alex was only 18. Unlike Kathleen Dehmlow, she didn't have any children to abandon. But in a Christian sense she did have children in the faith because she had led a lot of young people to Jesus Christ. Her legacy will live on in their lives, and they will never be abandoned because they will all live together for eternity!

Two ladies - two legacies - what will your legacy be?

LIFE LESSON

INFLUENCE THAT LIVES ON

THE SAVANNAH BANANAS

Baseball season is underway. Montgomery has a fine professional class AA baseball team, the Montgomery Biscuits. We are only a couple of hours away from the Atlanta Braves.

But our season began with a different brand of baseball. The Savannah Bananas came to play at Riverwalk Stadium. The stadium was totally sold out for two nights of baseball! I tried to use my influence, but couldn't get a ticket.

The Savannah Bananas are like the Harlem Globetrotters. They have some very talented ball players, but the whole purpose of their playing is not to excel in real baseball, but to entertain the crowd.

I realize that the more I learned about them, the more I saw a parallel to how life is lived today. Let me share seven similarities for you to think about:

1. The Savannah Bananas don't play by any set of rules-they make their own rules. If a foul ball goes in the stands and a fan catches it, it's an out. God gave us some rules in life that are very clear and concise-but many people don't follow the rules. They prefer just to make up their own rules. Life leads to a different result than a Savannah Bananas baseball game!

2. The players are very talented, but their talents are not used to play the legitimate game of baseball. They can catch fly balls in the

outfield between their legs. They can do cartwheels going down the baseline, Life is composed of very talented people, but some folks never use their talents for which they were created.

3. The umpires are a part of the entertainment. They intentionally make bad calls. They do interesting dances between pitches. Their purpose is to entertain, not to be in charge. God is the Chief Umpire in life. He doesn't play games. He has the best interest of every person at heart, and He is always right, just, and merciful.

4. The Bananas play strictly for entertainment. Their paychecks don't depend on their batting or fielding or how many runs they score. They are judged on how well they entertain. A lot of people see life strictly as entertainment. Anything goes as long as it is fun. That's vastly different from the productive, humble, disciplined, meek life to which God calls us to live.

5. The game is very entertaining but leaves a person empty. Jesus didn't come to make life entertaining, but to make life full, fresh, and forever.

6. The Savannah Bananas perform well in order to get a good paycheck. God didn't create life to be all about making a living. That's important, but our vocation ought to be used as a platform to serve God's people and to share the Good News. The purpose is quite different.

7. The Savannah Bananas always win. I'm sure sometimes it takes a lot of new rules and help from the umpires, etc., but they do win. In life, God's team is always going to win. The Book of Revelation makes it clear who will win, but there will be no rule adjustments and God has already offered His help through Jesus. To win or lose is your choice.

I plan to get myself a ticket early next year when they return to Montgomery, but I'm focusing more on life every day and being a part of God's team who does entertain, but who gives to each one of us a purpose to make every day count. When you live with Jesus Christ living in your heart, every day is a winning day!

Play ball!

LIFE LESSON

LIFE CAN BE FUN

WHAT DETERMINES YOUR DECISIONS?

Kristie Ennis is an above-the-knee amputee. She is a retired U.S. Marine Corps sergeant. In Afghanistan in 2012, she lost her left leg. Since then, she has taken up mountain climbing.

She has scaled six of the so-called "sevens summits" the highest peaks on the seven continents. She then tackled the big one-Mount Everest-but she was forced to turn back 200 meters from the peak of Mount Everest.

She and her team had been climbing for 43 days. Climbing is a huge challenge. She has to take a step with her right leg, then match it with her left leg, which is used to simply brace or stabilize her. One of the dangers is getting frostbite on her good limb because of the cold transferring so quickly through the aluminum and steel devices.

She is a winner. People wanted to know why she didn't finish the climb She was at the south summit. She could see the top of Everest, but she was having difficulty with her prosthetic device. If it went out, she didn't have the team to help her adequately. She knew that the team would be in jeopardy.

She decided to stop, not because she didn't think she could finish, but because she knew that she was putting the lives of a lot of people in danger. She said she wouldn't be able to live with herself if anybody on her team got hurt. She did say she would return and do it.

How many people make big decisions in life based on the welfare and safety of other people? How often do we think just of ourselves in making those decisions?

I have written about my great friend, Coach Jimmy Perry. After surviving cancer and heart surgery, he coached the St. James football team to a state championship in 2022-his first. He had one of the best quarterbacks in the state returning this year, along with several other stars. He had the inside track to win another state championship.

On a Monday night in February, a group of folks were discussing whether Jimmy would retire and asked me what I thought. I said that I doubted he would retire because he has developed these great players, and he will have another year with them. Early the next morning, Coach Perry called me to tell me that he had decided to announce his retirement later that morning.

I was surprised. He explained, "If I coached another year and won another championship, a lot of our seasoned players would graduate. Whoever replaced me would have a difficult time." He wanted to retire leaving great players for his successor so that they could be successful. His decision was based on not what he could accomplish for himself, but what he could do for somebody else.

Wow! How many of us think of others when we make big decisions? Kristie Ennis and Jimmy Perry did. Read about Esther, and Daniel, and Stephen, and Jesus. They did. Great American soldiers and leaders in the past did. They made decisions that cost them their lives so that our lives could be free, productive, and fulfilled!

LIFE LESSON

WHAT MOTIVATES THE DECISIONS YOU ARE MAKING NOW?

KOKO

My family and I moved to Montgomery in 1972 when I became pastor of Frazer. We lived for the first ten years in Carol Villa on Surrey Road. it was a great neighborhood with a lot of young people.

A special family in the neighborhood was Mr. and Mrs. Ben Curry. They lived just around the corner from us. Mr. Curry could fix anything. He loved helping Si and Vicki (and me) with anything that needed fixing.

Mr. Curry's son is Ashley Curry. Today, he is the Mayor of Vestavia Hills, Alabama. At his recent Mayor's Prayer Breakfast, his daughter Anna Gualano spoke. She has a powerful witness about dealing with the disease Osteogenesis Imperfecta (OI), also called brittle bone disease, where your bones break easily. She has had over 200 broken bones in her lifetime. She has experienced over 100 surgeries.

She gave one of the greatest speeches that I have heard about courage perseverance, and trusting in God. In her speech, she referred to an expression that her surgeon shared with her at every office visit and particularly after the many extensive surgeries performed by her doctor That expression was "Keep On Keeping On So, the letters KOKO became her mantra for overcoming obstacles. She still lives by that to this day. If you want to listen to her speech, follow this link https://www. youtube.com/watch?v=p0G-fT6HAOQ. It will inspire you.

When you set out to accomplish a goal, and things become challenging, you have two choices you can keep going forward or you can sit down and quit. Winners keep on keeping on-losers quit. Winners find a way-losers find an exit.

In his book, John Doe, Disciple, Peter Marshall talks about an assistant to Thomas Edison who was trying to find some way to console the legendary inventor because he had encountered so many failures in an important experiment. The assistant said, "It's too bad to do that much work without results." Mr. Edison quickly replied, "Oh, we have lots of results-we know 700 things that won't work!"

Edison knew that failure was not final, but simply an investment in the bank of knowledge of some things that didn't work. He said, "Our greatest weakness lies in giving up. The most certain way to success is always to try just one more time." He also said, "Many of life's failures are people who did not realize how close they were to success when they quit." Edison never quit!

I heard a cute story about a boy who was facing a tough situation in sports and wanted to quit. His father coached him by saying, "The people who are remembered in life are those who didn't quit." He said, "Remember Winston Churchill? He didn't quit. Remember Thomas Edison? He didn't quit. Remember George Washington Carver? He didn't quit." The boy nodded that he remembered all these people that his father had mentioned. Then his father said, "Remember John McKringle?" The boy looked puzzled and said, "No, who was he?" His father replied, "You see, you don't remember him - he quit."

Take quit out of your vocabulary. You never know what you might accomplish by taking the next step forward. Anna Gualano is a great example of always taking steps forward.

Paul reminds us "Good works always produce a harvest if we do not give up." (Galatians 6:9) James reminds us, "Anyone who meets a testing challenge head-on and manages to stick it out is mighty fortunate.... reward is life and more life." (James 1:12) David said, "Stay with God, take heart, don't quit." (Psalm 27:14)

K O K O – Keep On Keeping On!

LIFE LESSON

NEVER QUIT

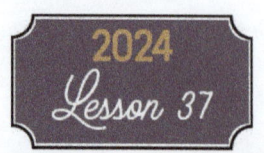

MEN'S MINISTRY-MUSEUM OR MOVEMENT

I attended five events during the month of July that were focused on a ministry to men. I believe it is one of the most critical ministries in which churches can be engaged to help men understand their role in the family, in society, in the church, and to commit their lives to Jesus who can make them the men they ought to be. I was inspired and encouraged at each of those events.

One was sponsored by Landmark Church of Christ. Each year they have a gridiron kick-off dinner. They could only accommodate 800 men. The tickets sold out in a few days. Landmark Church of Christ and their pastor, Buddy Bell, have a great desire to minister to all men in Montgomery. Tim Lee is a member there and for years has been able to get some of the best speakers anywhere.

One of the speakers was Cadillac Williams, who was an All American at Auburn. He had a great pro career and re-energized the Auburn fan base serving as interim head coach for four games in 2022. He is now the associate head coach at Auburn. I have written about his witness and how his mission was not only to win football games, but more importantly to win young people to become Christ followers. He did that as interim coach and is continuing to do that today.

The other speaker was Dan Orlovsky. He was a great quarterback in high school and college and played many years as a professional quarterback.

Today he is a part of the ESPN sports team calling games and hosting programs.

Dan really became famous last year when Demar Hamlin collapsed during a Buffalo Bills football game, and almost died. The whole nation's attention was focused on that situation. The game stopped and then was cancelled.

Dan Orlovsky was on the ESPN sports team covering that situation. He is a strong, bold Christian. He felt led to depart from the script and said that a lot of people had talked about how Demar was in their thoughts and prayers. He said that we ought not to talk about praying, but to pray. He asked his fellow ESPN team members on the set and tv audience to join him in praying. He knew he could get into a lot of trouble for praying-but he said that's what God told him to do, and he did it.

His prayer was powerful. He had not written out a prayer-he just prayed from his heart and everybody watching felt it. When Demar made a remarkable recovery months later, Dan made it clear that it was because of the prayers of many, many people across the world.

Dan told how he came to know Jesus in a personal way through other professional football players. He challenged each man to be sure that he is following Jesus, and that he is becoming a bold Godly husband and father and leader in society.

It's time for Men's Ministries to quit resembling a Museum and become a part of the Movement with a Mission! Are you and your church on the MMMMM team?

Live out William P. Merrill's hymn:

"Rise up, O men of God! Have done with lesser things; Give heart and soul and mind and strength To serve the King of kings."

LIFE LESSON

MUSEUM OR MOVEMENT?

HOW DO YOU HANDLE DEFEAT?

How do you handle defeats in life? Defeats do come. Nobody wins every time they go on the playing field, or business negotiations, or doctor's visit, or any venue in life. It's always fun to win, but how we handle defeat usually tells more about who we really are.

The third Saturday in October has become famous because Alabama plays Tennessee in football. It's an intense rivalry. The relationship between the fans of both schools is extremely competitive. In fact, it's despicable how some of the fans from each school talk about the other.

Alabama has had the upper hand for the past several years. In 2022, Tennessee was excited about changing that part of history. They did on Saturday, October 15, by winning 52-49.

Alabama had a stellar performance from its Heisman winning quarterback, Bryce Young. He is an exceptional young man. People weren't sure whether he would be able to play or not because of a shoulder injury. He took every Alabama snap.

Bryce is a great leader and a great football player, but he is even greater in his witness of the Christian faith. You will always see him before the game in the corner of the end zone, kneeling to pray. He doesn't do it for show he does it to acknowledge his commitment to God through Jesus Christ.

Bryce Young had a great game against Tennessee. He took a lot of punishment from the Tennessee defense. He never fussed at his teammates, complained to the referee, or lost his cool.

How would Bryce Young handle defeat? He sent out the following message the day after the Tennessee loss, which demonstrates the kind of winner he is:

"If you want us to cry-we will not. If you're looking for excuses there are none at the University of Alabama. Tired & Weary, but never broken. The things you learn from losses are far more important than those moments when you're standing on the mountain top. Romans 5:3-5 says, "More than that, we rejoice in our sufferings, knowing that suffering produces endurance, and endurance produces character, and character produces hope, and hope does not put us to shame, because God's love has been poured into our hearts through the Holy Spirit who has been given to us." Win, lose or tie, I'm Alabama 'til I die. If you haven't given up on the Tide, go grab a jersey!

When a person loses, he has a lot of options of how to handle it. Some people quit-some people complain some people have a pity partysome blame it on the referees or the weather conditions, etc. Bryce Young handled defeat using a Biblical perspective. That's the best way to handle defeat!

I have a hunch that Bryce Young will be a better leader than ever. He has often times stood on the mountain top-he also knows how to go through the valley. He doesn't stay in the valley-he goes through it! (Psalm 23:4) It will be interesting to see the next mountain top that he conquers.

How do you handle defeat?

LIFE LESSON

HOW TO DEAL WITH DEFEAT

LET'S PRAY!

On Monday, January 2, 2023, one of the most important NFL games of the year was just ten minutes into the first quarter. The outcome of this game between the Buffalo Bills and Cincinnati Bengals would influence the playoff status of several teams.

An unexpected thing happened. Buffalo Bills safety, Damar Hamlin, tackled Bengals Dee Higgins. Damar got up, took a couple of steps, and then collapsed on the field because of cardiac arrest.

The medical teams from both sidelines were on the field immediately and started medical procedures including CPR. After 30 minutes, they placed Damar in an ambulance and carried him to a Cincinnati hospital.

Prayer was primary for most every person. Nobody was debating whether or not you should have prayer at a football game or that players could kneel and pray. ESPN analyst, Dan Orlovsky, told viewers nationwide, "Maybe this is not the right thing to do, but I want to." He said that the Buffalo Bills organization believes in prayer. He prayed, "If we believed prayer didn't work, we wouldn't ask this of you God. We believe in prayer....." Marcus Spears and Laura Rutledge said, "Amen" Google the whole prayer that he prayed.

People have continued to pray around Buffalo, New York, Cincinnati and everywhere. It is reported that people meet on street corners, public places, and designated venues, and circle up and pray. I think Damar is the most prayed for person in America!

This event has re-enforced many beliefs and commitments for me. Here are two that I will share:

1. Prayer is primary. It's sad that we have to get in situations like this to remind us of the importance of prayer. We must learn that we don't have to get on our backs before we need to look up.

   The Bible says that sincere, passionate prayer of a righteous person avails much. (James 5:16) Mark records the healing of a young boy by Jesus. When the disciples questioned why they couldn't heal him, Jesus said, "This kind can come out only by prayer." (Mark 9:29)

   Practice praying daily and experience the power of prayer every day this year.

2. Remember what's important in life. At the beginning of the football game, everybody thought that game was one of the most important issues in life. Ten minutes into the game nobody thought that football was nearly as important as the life and health of a young 24-year-old ball player.

   The coaches were reminded of that lesson during the time that doctors were administering to Damar on the field. Bengals Coach Zac Taylor and Bills Coach Sean McDermott were standing with their arms around each other. It was still undecided if the game would be resumed. McDermott told Taylor, "If they resume the game, I am not coaching it. I'm going to the hospital with my player, Damar."

Begin each day in 2023 answering the question, "What and who is most important in my life?" Don't get your values inverted. Read Matthew 6:33 and Matthew 22:37.

Everyday experience: Prayer-Power-Priorities-Possibilities

LIFE LESSON

THE POWER OF PRAYER

81

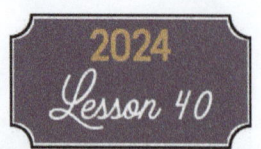

TODAY

ESPN loves Montgomery. While a lot of different cities would like to have a bowl game, Montgomery has two! We just completed the Camellia Bowl on Tuesday, December 27, 2022.

I serve on the River Region Sports Commission. This group initiates and promotes sporting events throughout the River Region. Our key person is Johnny Williams, who has a great relationship with ESPN. The chairman of the commission is Dr. Karl Stegall.

The Camellia Bowl featured the Buffalo Bulls playing the Georgia Southern Eagles. It was a beautiful day, and we had a huge crowd. The east stands were full.

Buffalo played under tremendous adversity. They left Buffalo, New York at midnight on Thursday in order to get ahead of the huge blizzard. The band, cheerleaders, school officials, and fans were not as fortunate. They got snowed in and were unable to come south for the game.

Buffalo has a great coaching staff and team members. One thing they do is have a team chapel the night before each game. The person who does their team chapel was grounded in Buffalo. The coaches inquired about someone to do the chapel and Karl suggested me. I accepted.

Tim Lee and I went about 30 minutes early to the Renaissance Hotel. The head coach, Mo Linguist, asked us to sit down and talk with him. He had a lot of responsibilities, but we spent 30 minutes before the team chapel talking about life and how to make a difference in the world and we all prayed together.

The coach told me a lot about his faith journey. He begins every team meeting by placing in big letters on a PowerPoint one word-TODAY. They talk about forgetting yesterday and not trying to live in tomorrow, but how is God going to use them today to fulfill His purpose for their lives. He says "TODAY" and they repeat back to him "TODAY." They do it several times.

You can guess how I started my devotional. I looked at them and smiled and said, "TODAY. You could see their faces brighten up and they all said "TODAY" I shared with them how God has a plan and purpose for their life-TODAY.

Coach Mo shared that it's tough being in Montgomery, Alabama when your family, friends, and fans are back in Buffalo, New York. He shared with me a picture of his wife and three kids. They just had a new baby son born the day before the team left for Montgomery! The baby was in the picture.

Despite the adversity, Buffalo beat Georgia Southern 23-21! The post-game celebration on the field was special. When ESPN interviewed Coach Mo, the first thing he said was, "We give the glory to God." When they interviewed the player who was selected as the most valuable player, he began by saying, "I want to thank God and give Him the glory. In accepting the Camellia Bowl trophy, Coach Mo thanked Montgomery, the appropriate officials, etc., and then even thanked Reverend Mathison for speaking to his team!

It was a great experience for me to meet a group of college coaches and players who were doing it right! They were polite, humble, talented, competitive, and ready to give God the glory.

2023-TODAY-Paul said, "Forget those things which are behind and reach forth for the things that are before you and press on toward the mark of God's high calling for your life." (Philippians 3:13,14) Follow that plan and you will be a winner!

LIFE LESSON

TODAY IS THE DAY

FOLLOW THE LEADER

The TBK Bank Quad Cities Marathon is a Boston qualifier course. The 26.2 mile-run starts and ends in downtown Moline, Illinois. It carries the runners through some of the most picturesque scenes of our nation's heartland.

In the September 2021 race, a very unusual thing happened. Tyler Pence is a sports coach at the University of Illinois. During the race, he was far behind two Kenyan runners. Because the Kenyans were so fast, volunteer leaders were not in place yet to direct the runners. A volunteer leader unintentionally directed the Kenyan runners to make a wrong turn. Because of the extra mileage they ran, Tyler Pence won the race. It was the first time a local person had won in many years.

This happens occasionally. In the Venice marathon in 2017, a local Italian runner won the race when the six leading runners took a wrong turn. It is very important to have leaders who can lead. People follow where leaders lead.

When I was pastor at Frazer, we had a large children's choir program. One Sunday night, the 5-year-old children's choir was going to sing at the evening worship service. There were 49 of them present. They lined up in the hall outside the Sanctuary so they could come in at the appropriate time to sing.

The teachers had done an excellent job in teaching the music. They made one simple error in picking the wrong little boy to be the leader. He had on a new suit and bowtie, and everybody thought he was cute.

The little boy started leading the other 48 children down the side aisle. people sitting in the pews were smiling and commenting about how cute he looked. He began to enjoy it. Rather than leading the children up to the steps to sing, he just took a right turn near the altar rail and started back up the center aisle. All 48 were following him. His mother saw what was happening but was not sitting on the end of the pew. She tried to grab him but was unable to.

I'll never forget the scene of those 49 children going up and down the aisles following that little boy. Finally, his daddy intercepted him on the second trip around and led him up to the steps. The rest of the kids followed. People follow where leaders lead.

The problem in many churches is that leaders are being complimented and enjoying their leadership role but deviate from the course they should be leading. Some churches just go around in circles because they are following the leader.

When business organizations, churches, athletic teams, and schools get the right leader, you begin to see amazing results. Observe the leadership in any organization in which you are a part. Is it being led by people you want to follow?

Moses invited the children of Israel to follow him to the Promised Land. They followed. (Exodus 6 ff.) Nehemiah invited the people to join him in rebuilding the walls of Jerusalem. They followed him. (Nehemiah 2,3 #) Jesus invited people to follow him, and they did. (Matthew 4:18-22) People follow where leaders lead.

The most important race in town is the race of life. Are you leading people to win an imperishable prize? (I Corinthians 9:24-27) Are you following leaders who are leading to the finish line?

LIFE LESSON

THE IMPORTANCE OF GOOD LEADERSHIP

A TALL MAN STANDS TALL!

Wesley Britt is one of the great Christian athletes to grow up in Alabama. His faith helped him in so many aspects of his life, God always had first place.

Wesley is a good-sized boy-6 feet 8 inches tall and had a playing weight of 320 pounds. He was an All-American at the University of Alabama and played for the New England Patriots for several years.

After professional football, he served as Director of Economic Community Development with Alabama Power. He earned advanced degrees. Recently he joined the firm, Fine Geddie and Associates.

Wesley always had his priorities in order. When asked about his development as a Christian, he says that his most important role that God has for him is to be a good husband to his wife Katie and a good dad to his children Bennett and Ridgeway. That speaks volumes about values.

He started for forty-six straight football games at the University of Alabama. His consecutive starts of a game were broken only when he broke his leg against Tennessee.

Wes was heavily recruited by several SEC schools. He almost went to Florida. He had always been an Auburn fan, but the position coach told him he didn't think he could play in the SEC. Big mistake!! He went to Alabama because of the integrity and Christian witness of the coach recruiting him-Dabo Swinney.

It's most interesting to me that there was one group that named him for their All-American team, but with a condition. Playboy magazine said that he would be on their All-American team if he would be willing to have his picture and name appear in the Playboy magazine. Wesley said "No." He refused to have his picture and name linked to Playboy. Wouldn't it be great if more athletes stood up and expressed their values?

When he was playing with New England and going to the Super Bowl, he helped readjust the player personnel for that game. Wesley agreed to play tight end-something he had never done before. He knew offensive tackle. He thought this might be an opportunity for him to catch a pass and score a touchdown. In all his football history, he had never scored a touchdown. He wondered how much he should beg Tom Brady to throw the ball to him. Then he remembered that Coach Bear Bryant always told the team, "When you score, act like you've been there before" Wes didn't know how he might act because he had never been there before.

Wes is a tall man physically, but he is a much taller man spiritually. He stands tall for the right things in the Christian faith. Lynn and I had an opportunity to pray with him and Katie at a public gathering in the early days for her run for the U.S. Senate. To pray with them and for them was a great privilege.

I recently sat with Wes and Wayne Atcheson, former SID for Alabama, at a piano concert featuring Wayne's brother Randall. I volunteered to be the bodyguard for Wes that night! He felt safe!

Wes stands tall in every way! He is the kind of Christian that young people can look up to and follow! His wife, Senator Katie Britt, is also a powerful role model for people of all ages.

How tall are you?

LIFE LESSON

THE REAL MEANING OF STANDING TALL

A TRADE THAT MADE HEADLINES

When you are a baseball pitcher, there are a lot of different ways to get your name in the headlines. You can pitch a no-hitter, have a perfect game, strike out a lot of people, have an enviable win/loss record, have the best fastball or curve-those are headliners. A few years ago, there were two left-handed pitchers who made headlines for a different reason.

The biggest trade headline in 1973 occurred in the New York Yankees spring training camp in Fort Lauderdale when Mike Kekich and Fritz Peterson announced a trade-they had decided to swap wives, two children apiece, and even family dogs. The announcement of that trade traveled faster than any other trade in baseball!

Both families have been friends since 1969. They lived in New Jersey. The children were about the same age. They actually went to family events together. At some time during the 1972 season, each of them became interested in the marriage partner of the other couple. When they announced the trade, the baseball commissioner was "appalled," but couldn't interfere. He received more mail about that trade than he did about the introduction of the designated hitter!

One interesting moment occurred when the Yankees General Manager, Lee MacPhail, cracked, "We may have to call off Family Day!"

Neither Kekich nor Peterson will ever make it to the Hall of Fame-but they both saw that they had made the Hall of Shame. That's what they will be remembered for.

If you want to get your name in the headlines, pursue something good that makes a difference. You can make the headlines by robbing a bank, cheating people out of money, making a public spectacle of yourself-or you can make a difference by giving to people in need, serving the underserved in the community, living your life serving God's Kingdom. These might not make the human headlines, but they'll make the heavenly headlines!

If you're interested in some kind of trade, the first trade should be to trade in your old self and receive the new self that God wants to create. "When a person becomes a Christian, he becomes a brand new person...A new life has begun." (II Corinthians 5:17)

Trade in a negative attitude for a positive attitude. That will improve your life and the lives of all the people around you. "Have this attitude in yourselves which was also in Christ Jesus" (Philippians 2:5)

Trade a "getting" mentality for a "giving" mentality. We discover many more blessings in giving. "It is more blessed to give than to receive." (Acts 20:35)

Trade bad choices for good choices. Every choice has a consequence that will determine your direction in life. Choose who to serve. "But as for me and my household, we will serve the LORD" (Joshua 24:15)

Trading spouses, children, and dogs are not God's plan. You will win at the game of life if you make the right trades in life in order to follow His plan!

Be very selective in every trade that you make!

LIFE LESSON

TRADING CAN PRODUCE MIXED RESULTS

PAY OR PLATFORM

I once heard a successful man who had gone up the ladder in a company giving advice to a group of young people who were just employed. He said, "The way to be successful is to figure out who is boss, and please the boss."

There is a degree of truth in that, but I think a greater truth in under. standing our work is that we are here to please God, not a boss. Being successful is not just going up higher in the company but discovering how to please God by using our work as a platform to do His ministry.

Paul writes, "Work hard cheerfully in all you do just as though you are working for the Lord, not merely for your employers. Remember that it is the Lord Jesus who is going to pay you, giving you a full portion of all He owns. He is really the one you are working for. If you don't give your best for Him, He will pay you in a way you don't like." (Colossians 3:23 MSG)

The purpose of our work is to please God. Many people talk about getting tired at work. There is a degree of physical exhaustion, but a great source of energy is knowing that we are connected to God to receive His strength in doing what He has called us to do.

Harvard Business Review said that many corporations assume that younger workers have more energy and are therefore more productive. Age is not the determining factor. More people under the age of 45 (43%) say they are exhausted at work than those over 45 (35%). Now get this-they found that the least exhausted workers are those over 60!

I saw a cartoon recently where the boss walks up behind a young employee who was deeply engrossed in playing a game on his phone. The boss said, "Why aren't you working?" The man looked at him and said, "Sir, I just didn't see you coming."

There are a lot of people who are willing to work if the boss is watching. Good employees do their work whether the boss is watching or not because God is always watching, and they work to please God.

Martin Luther once said, "A Christian shoemaker does his duty not by putting little crosses on the shoes, but by making good shoes, because God is interested in good craftsmanship." A work ethic that is motivated by a desire to please God will produce excellent work.

A great golfer emerged this year, Scottie Scheffler. He won the Masters and has been the #1 ranked golfer in the world. Following his victory at the Masters, he was asked at a press conference how he balances his fierce desire to compete without allowing it to define who he is as a person. He replied, "The reason why I play golf is I am trying to glorify God and all that He has done in my life. So, for me, my identity isn't a golf course."

He continued, "My wife, Meredith, told me this morning, if you win this golf tournament today, if you lose this golf tournament by ten shots, if you never win another golf tournament again, I am still going to love you and you're still going to be the same person. Jesus loves you and nothing changes." Scheffler then said, "All I am trying to do is glorify God and that's why I'm here and that's why I am in this position." Golf is his platform for ministry!

Is your job about pay or platform?

LIFE LESSON

WHO YOU SHOULD PLEASE

REAL WINNERS

One of the great coaches who attends the FCA Family Coaches Confer. once every year with her family is Cindy Hawthorne from Brantley, Alabama. She just won her third straight softball championship. She has won six in the last ten years. She is a strong Christian and gives all the glory to God.

The most dominant college girls' softball team is the Oklahoma Sooners. Their record this year was 61-1. That's the best ever! They just won their third consecutive national championship. I followed their progress, partly because of their success, but more because of their Christian witness.

The players were interviewed after winning their third consecutive Natty. They immediately gave all the praise and glory to Jesus Christ.

Their theme has been "eyes up." Whenever they make a good play or score a run, they put their fingers near their eyes and look up to say they are "fixing our eyes on Jesus."

Grace Lyon was asked what their secret is for maintaining joy and energy through a long season. She replied, "Our joy comes from the Lord and it's really the only thing that can keep you motivated and in a good mindset no matter the outcome." Immediately, other players said, "We agree one thousand percent with Grace."

One of the interviewers said, "It's very obvious that the Lord is at work on this team."

Jayda Coleman said that she was not a Christian when she was a freshman, and they won her first national championship. She was happy for few days but didn't feel joy. When she surrendered her life to Christ, the experienced real joy.

She said, "I think that's what makes our team so strong is that we are not afraid to lose because it's not the end of the world if we do lose. Yes, we worked our butts off to be here and we want to win, but it's not the end of the world because our life is in Christ and that's all that matters."

Patty Gasso is the head coach. She credits God with changing her mindset a few years ago from a focus on winning softball games to winning souls. God said to her, "You open the door and let them in, and I'll take over from there." This was Gasso's seventh national title!

Alyssa Brito witnessed how Christ changed her life. She said that they wanted to win, but if they did not win, they would really win in life and eternity. She said, "This isn't our home. We have an eternity of joy with our Father and I'm so excited about that."

The Brantley High School girls' team and the Oklahoma Sooners girls' team both know how to win on the diamond and in life. They concentrate on trying to get home to score a run, but they are more interested in taking people with them to their real home which is in Heaven. Now that's what I call real winners!

Coaches have such a great opportunity. That's the reason I enjoy spending time with coaches and speaking at coach's conferences each year. They have a huge platform.

LIFE LESSON

HOW ARE YOU USING YOUR PLATFORM?

TWO GREAT CHRISTIAN ATHLETES

When I finished seminary at Candler School of Theology in 1963, my roommate and I decided to go to an ivy league school for another graduate degree. I went to Princeton Seminary.

At that time, Bill Bradley was a great basketball player at Princeton University. After Princeton, he went on to play for the New York Knicks and won two world championships and was an all-pro basketball player. He then was elected as Senator for New Jersey in 1979 and served until 1997.

Bill Bradley and I became casual friends at Princeton because he was considering playing basketball for the Venture for Victory basketball team on which I had played two years before. It is now known as Athletes in Action. The team plays international Olympic teams and colleges and gives a Christian witness.

Don Moomaw was the first two-time All-American football player at UCLA. He was 6'4" weighed 200 pounds. He was a great athlete. He was an even greater Christian witness.

Following his great college and professional career as a football player, he became a Presbyterian minister. He received his training at Princeton Seminary and went back to California to become senior pastor at the First Presbyterian Church of Hollywood and the Bel Air Presbyterian Church of Los Angeles. President Ronald Reagan was a member of his congregation.

Moomaw was deeply committed to the Fellowship of Christian Athletes. He served as the national president of the FCA. He wrote a great article about Bill Bradley. Here is a portion of that article:

"A Russian track star gave me a doll," said tall, rugged Princeton basketball star Bill Bradley, "so I gave him a Russian New Testament." Why would this star-forward of the U.S.A. Olympic basketball team present the New Testament as a gift? His answer: "It's the most important thing in the world to me."

As Bradley tells his story, it all began when his mother read in a Sunday supplement about the Fellowship of Christian Athletes. She encouraged him to attend the movement's annual summer conference. His counselor there was Fran Tarkenton, quarterback of the Minnesota Vikings and a dedicated Christian.

"I had an intellectual belief," Bradley continued, "but it had never filtered down to take possession of my heart and my emotions. I don't mind telling you when God in Christ came into my heart, I got emotional. I knew it was real."

The Bible helped Bradley through spiritual frustration during freshman days at Princeton, where he "got into a small Bible study of concerned students and really began to grow."

What has been Bill Bradley's greatest thrill in the Olympics? Not the opening ceremonies, when 5,000 athletes from all nations saw the Olympic torch lighted; not when Bradley won his first game against Australia. "No, the greatest thrill of the Olympics for me has been meeting Christians from other nations," says the two-time All-American basketball player. "For example, I met the coach of the Nigerian track team. He is an outstanding believer, won to Christ by a faithful mother and father who had become Christians through some courageous missionaries. This is a great family we are in."

Two great Christian athletes-Bill Bradley and Don Moomaw. I have been inspired by both of them.

What inspires you?

LIFE LESSON

CELEBRATING THE MOST IMPORTANT VICTORIES

ERIC LIDDELL'S BOLD STAND

One of the most awesome movies I ever saw was Chariots of Fire. It was both convicting and inspiring. It represented an athlete who was willing to give up an almost guaranteed gold medal in the Olympics to stand up for his Christian convictions.

Eric Liddell was born in China where his parents were serving as missionaries. In that day, children were often enrolled in boarding schools outside of China. Eric was sent to a boarding school in London, It wasn't long before it was obvious that he had athletic skills in running and rugby.

One hundred years ago, 1924, he was a sure bet to win the 100-meter race in the Olympics, but a problem occurred when the schedule showed that the 100-meter race would be run on Sunday.

Eric Liddell was a committed Christian. He could easily have found reasons to try and have the race changed to a different time. He had influential people who could appeal to the Olympic Committee to change the date for the 100-meters. He could have rationalized that he could attend worship on Sunday morning, because the race was not run until Sunday afternoon. He probably considered those and many other alternatives. But he was convicted that his commitment to Christ would not allow him to run on Sunday. Therefore, he made a bold stand for his Christian convictions!

A friend offered Eric his spot in the 400 meters. Eric was not so good at that because of the distance, but he began working hard to become a 400-meter runner. He improved every day.

Part of running the 400-meters a hundred years ago was to pace yourself for part of the race and then use the last two hundred meters for a big kick. Liddell knew that he was not as strong as the other runners to finish with a big kick. He decided he had to run the whole race as a sprint. Nobody had done that at that time.

Liddell ran the race his way-full speed. He finished it in 47.6 seconds for a new world record!

Eric Liddell was a hero to me because he had the courage to stand up for what he believed was right. His greatest goal was not to win an Olympic Gold Medal, but to be sure that people knew that his Christian walk was consistent with his Christian talk. A hundred years later, has there ever been a more important time for Christians to exemplify that?

The 2024 Olympics introduced a lot of highly controversial issues, such as the role of drag queens, sexual implications, and potentially making fun of Christian rituals. What would Eric Liddell do if he was running in the 2024 Olympics? I know that he would stand firm in his convictions to also show that the Christian way is a better way. Read Romans 12:1,2.

Christianity was ridiculed in a lot of ways in the 2024 Olympics. Why should Christians be appalled at this? The percentage of Christians in France and the world is very low. We can complain about what we saw, or feel sorry for ourselves, or we can follow Eric Liddell's lead and stand up for what we believe!

Eric Liddell can teach us how we can handle the 2024 Olympics. Like him, I know that Christianity is going to ultimately win. The Book of Revelation is a huge scoreboard that says, "JESUS WINS."

Are you willing, like Eric Liddell, to stand up today?

LIFE LESSON

COURAGEOUS CONVICTIONS

OLYMPIC LESSONS

Here are five lessons we can learn from the 2024 Olympics:

1. Discipline-It takes discipline to be a good athlete, but to compete at the highest level in the world requires extreme discipline. Winners must have extreme discipline.

   How many of us are that disciplined about our Christian witness? How disciplined are we in prayer and Bible study? How disciplined are we in carrying out the commands of Christ?

2. Margin of victory so many of the events at the Olympics were settled by an extremely small margin of victory. In almost every sport winners won because they had a little something extra to give to create that slight margin of victory. The Men's 100-meter race determines the fastest man on the planet. Noah Lyles of the USA won by 5/1000th of a second!

   How much are we willing to invest to carry out God's purpose for our life? The margin of victory might be extremely small am I willing to give the extra effort? The people who gave the greatest effort at the correct time were the ones who emerged as winners. Jesus taught, "If someone forces you to go one mile, go with that person two miles" (Matthew 5:41) The mile that means the most in life is always the extra effort mile!

3. Obstacles overcome I was amazed at the number of stories of athletes who had overcome severe obstacles just to be able to compete in the Olympics. I remember those pictures of the early childhood of some of the athletes who grew up in deplorable conditions, but the obstacles did not stop them.

   You will have obstacles in life. Choose to trust Christ to help you overcome your obstacles. Paul said, "I can do all things through Christ who strengthens me. (Philippians 4:13)

4. Gold medal value while we call them gold medals, they are not actually gold. They are only gold plated. The amount of gold in the gold medal is just 1,34%. The medals have not actually been gold since the 1912 Stockholm games.

   The real value is not in the medal itself, but in what it stands for. In life the things we think are "gold" are just gold plated-not the real thing. Gold plated temptations have been around since the Garden of Eden game.

5. The burning torch-it is always a spectacular event when the Olympic torch is lighted. It is kept a secret, and every host country tries to do something more creative and spectacular than the other host countries. The flame stays lit for the entirety of the games.

   Jesus said that we are the light of the world. Our light is not something that is to be turned on and off at our convenience. What God desires is consistency. Too often we have moments when the flames of our faith are dimmed or go out. Jesus said, "Let your light so shine before men that they may see your good works and glorify your Father who is in heaven." (Matthew 5:16)

The most important lesson is not the final score of any event in the Olympics, but the final score of our lives as we strive to win at the most important game in town life. You can win five times as many Olympic medals as Simone Biles, and still be miserable. The best way to win in life is not to try to get more medals but to lose our self in serving Christ. Read Matthew 16:24-26. That is the big lesson!

You can be a real winner!

LIFE LESSON

GOING FOR THE GOLD

THE POWER OF PURPOSE

Mark Twain said that there are two most important days in your life- the first is the day that you were born, and the second is the day that you know why you were born.

The sports world saw this demonstrated in the past few weeks with the life of a quarterback for the University of Alabama. Jalen Milroe was a starter at the first of the season. He had a couple of bad games and was benched. Alabama fans were ready to put him in the transfer portal.

Then, the offensive coordinator redesigned some of the offense around the gifts that he had. He began to flourish. He came back as a starter and Alabama won the rest of their games.

Alabama was trailing Auburn with a few seconds left and had 4th and 31 yards. The sports predictors indicated that Alabama would have a .01% chance of scoring. But Milroe knew his purpose. When you know your purpose, .01% is adequate. Alabama scored and won.

Then Alabama went against the number one team in the nation, the Georgia Bulldogs, who had a 29-game winning streak. Alabama came back to win that game and Milroe was the most valuable player.

How did this happen in two straight games? Following the Auburn game, he was questioned by reporters about how he overcame being benched, then coming back. What was his secret? He made this statement, "I had my purpose before they had their opinion."

In the championship game, he was interviewed twice, first on the field following the game and then on the platform receiving the Most Valuable Player trophy. Both times he was asked the secret of overcoming almost impossible odds. Twice he answered, "I had my purpose before they had their opinion." That's the power of purpose!

He wasn't the first Alabama quarterback to make that statement this year. Jalen Hurts had been the quarterback at Alabama, then was also benched, and eventually he transferred to Oklahoma. He went on to have a great career and was drafted by the Philadelphia Eagles. He could be the most valuable player in the National Football League this year!

He also was asked that question about how he could overcome so many adversities. He gave the same answer, "Before they had their opinions, I had my purpose." That's the power of purpose!

I just had a new book published last week on this very topic. It's entitled, "Why Am I Here." It's 54 life lessons to help everybody answer that question.

When you know your purpose, it makes other decisions easy. If you don't know your purpose, you do a lot of guessing about what you ought to do. Derric Johnson says, "If you have a WHY in life, you can always find a HOW!"

The book was published by my ministry for $10.00. It can be purchased at Henig Furs, Adams Drugs, the Locker Room, Mathison Interiors in Auburn, the Frazer bookstore, and our office which is in Henig Furs. If you would like to order one, the cost is $10.00 plus postage.

Do you know why you are here? As Milroe and Hurts would say, "I had my purpose before they had their opinion." Discover the power of purpose!

Do you have your purpose?

LIFE LESSON

PURPOSE PACKS POWER

THE JUNGLE

College basketball coaches say that one of the toughest places to play is in the Neville Arena in Auburn. It's referred to as "The Jungle." Rece Davis of ESPN said that the intensity is as good as anything you will see anywhere.

Homecourt advantage has always been important in basketball. Normally it's considered to be worth about two points. The Jungle has raised that bar to where it's conceded that homecourt advantage in The Jungle is about six plus points.

The Jungle didn't just happen-it is organized. Fifteen Auburn students make up "The Jungle staff." They meet weekly to discuss everything from merchandise distribution to crowd control methods to see that The Jungle runs as smoothly as possible. Their goal is to ensure that game days are always enjoyable for Auburn students and they help. Auburn win.

The "King" of The Jungle is its president Grayson Harbin. His leadership has raised The Jungle to a new level. He says his greatest satisfaction is "seeing how much of an impact we have made not only of men's basketball but other sports we handle as well. We have broken attendance records at both women's basketball and volleyball this year."

The Jungle is not the first reference to the advantage of playing for a home crowd. Hebrews 12:1 uses the backdrop of an athletic event, a race, to describe how people can win in the game of life. They were running in front of a huge group of fans who were pulling for them. Read Hebrews 11 and you see a litany of great heroes of the faith who are in Heaven pulling for and cheering on every person who is running for the home team.

The home court is an advantage because athletes perform better when an atmosphere is created where they are encouraged, cheered for, and hear chants that express encouragement to them. In life, we need to remember that we have that same home court advantage as the great Biblical heroes who have gone before us and are cheering for us.

I hope you are a part of some kind of small group, accountability group, or people who are cheering for you to become all that God wants you to be. This is a day of spiritual warfare. Satan is trying to win your life and he is most effective when he gets you by yourself. He will outsmart you in one-on-one situations. But if you are a part of a community-a supportive group, Satan has to go against not only God but also a group of people who are on your team. He can't deal with that.

Two of my favorite church members at Frazer were Tommy Neville, who was an all-pro lineman with the New England Patriots, and Mike Kolen, who was an all-pro linebacker for the Miami Dolphins when they went undefeated and won the Super Bowl. There are some places in Montgomery that I would not go by myself at night. They are not safe. But I was willing to go anywhere in Montgomery at any time of the day or night with Tommy and Mike because I knew that I was with a couple of guys who would not only cheer me on but would protect me.

The most important game in town is the game of your life. Every day you can know that you have God and his people surrounding you to encourage, convict, and inspire you. That is Satan's biggest obstacle and your greatest asset!

Organize your Jungle!

LIFE LESSON

CHECK YOUR SURROUNDINGS

THE REAL OLYMPIAN WINNERS

The highest visibility sporting event this year was the 2024 Olympic Games in Paris. Many Christians participated and won medals. It's easy to remember the negative things you saw and heard, but let me help us focus on the positive witness of some Christians.

My good friend, Wayne Atcheson, helped start the Fellowship of Christian Athletes huddle at the University of Alabama, the longest running huddle group in America. He served as Sports Information Director at Alabama and later went to Charlotte at Billy Graham's request to oversee the Billy Graham Library. He shared some Christian quotes in a devotion for the employees at the Billy Graham Association. I've added a few to his list.

- Sydney McLaughlin-Levrone won a gold medal and set a new world record in track. She said, "Records come and go but the glory of God is eternal. I no longer run for self-recognition but to reflect His perfect will that is already set in stone. I don't deserve anything, but by grace through faith, Jesus has given me everything."

- The Fijian Olympians sang four-part harmony hymns in the Olympian Village every morning and every evening. A moving moment was when the rugby team sang a hymn prior to their game. The Fiji athletes were asked where they learned those hymns and four-part harmony and they said, "Our families taught them to us during our time of family devotions and in our churches each Sunday."

- Scottie Scheffler, gold medal winner and the number one golfer in the world, said, "The reason why I play golf is I am trying to glorify God and all He has done in my life. So, for me, my identity is not on a golf course or a gold medal."

- Kennedy Blades, a USA wrestler, said to NBC, "I'm going to be honest; I've just gotten super close to Jesus. He is King and He's coming soon. So, I really believe if you guys put your heart into Jesus Christ, you guys will experience nothing but happiness and grace."

- Steph Curry, who set records for the most 3-pointers for the gold medal USA team, said, "For me to get a gold medal is insane, and I thank God for the opportunity to experience it"

- While the Olympic Committee does not allow the display of religious signs, the Brazilian bronze medal winner, Rayssa Leal, when she received her medal in skateboard, smiled at the camera and sent a message in sign language, "Jesus is the way, the truth, and the life."

- USA's Aaron Brooks had "100% Jesus" on a headband he wore during his wrestling success.

- USA had its first male gymnast medal in years. Brody Malone had to overcome many dark trials and a broken leg. He said, "Not to us, Lord, not to us, but to your name we give glory because of your faithful love, because of your truth."

- A young Christian soccer player from a nation that has a lot of Christian persecution, wore a t-shirt with the words "Jesus Revealed, Jesus Glorified, Haleluya."

What's your quote about your faith?

LIFE LESSON

KEEPING SCORE GOD'S WAY

AN INTERESTING INTRODUCTION

Faulkner University has a major event each year with an outstanding speaker. This year the event will be held on October 3, 2024 and Coach Nick Saban will be the speaker. It was a sellout immediately.

Coach Gene Stallings was invited to introduce Coach Saban. Coach Stallings is now 90 years old and lives on his 600-acre ranch in Paris, Texas. He said he would accept the invitation, but someone would have to come out to Paris, Texas and film the introduction. Montgomery was too far away.

My good friend Tim Lee is a long-time friend of Coach Stallings. Tim played basketball at Faulkner. Tim invited a friend who had a plane to fly him and a film crew from Faulkner to Paris, Texas.

When Tim asked how he was doing, Coach Stallings indicated that he was doing better than he had been doing recently. He said that a couple of weeks before, two of his donkeys were not where they should have been late in the afternoon. Since they were favorites of his family, he decided to go out and find them.

It wasn't long before he was at a distant point on the ranch and decided he had better start for home. It was so dark that he couldn't see his hand in front of his face or find a path or a way to get home. He decided to spend the night sleeping on the ground.

Immediately, a lot of people went out searching the ranch all night to try and find Coach Stallings. Early the next morning, just as the sun was peeking over the horizon, Coach Stallings said he heard some of the best words he had ever heard when a couple of the searchers shouted out, "There he is, there he is and he's okay." Coach Stallings jokingly said, "I knew where I was all of the time."

If you attend the gala event at the Renaissance Hotel and see the video of the introduction, just view it in the context that it could have been a tragic event.

It makes me wonder about the future. We all think we have a lot of days to live. Coach Stallings was on his own ranch, and he never dreamed that he would get lost and spend the night on the ground. My first thought was that some animal might have attacked him. I have watched him coach enough to know him that any animal would be foolish to try to take on Coach Stallings!

Coach Stallings followed another great Alabama coach nicknamed Bear Bryant because one day he had to fight a bear. If Coach Stallings had to fight a wild animal while he was looking for his donkeys, we might have seen another Alabama Coach get a nickname for being victorious over a huge animal. If that wild animal had been a tiger, I doubt Coach Stallings would have wanted to be called "Tiger Stallings."

I hope that someday when you die you will spend eternity with Jesus, I hope you see the sun coming up and I hope you hear Him saying, "There he is. He's alive. He's okay." Your life in this world is important, but being alive for eternity in God's Kingdom is the greatest victory anybody can ever win.

if you don't know where you are today and you can't find your way. know that darkness doesn't hinder God in finding you. He has a room prepared for you in Heaven! He won't stop searching until He offers to take you to His house. (Read John 14:1-7)

Wake up. What do you hear today?

LIFE LESSON

A 90-YEAR-OLD COACH WHO STILL CARES ABOUT DONKEYS

QUOTABLE QUOTES

Forgiveness doesn't change the past, but it does change the future.

Genuine kamikaze pilots don't plan their next sortie.

A thousand times a baby has become a king-but only once has a King become a baby.

The first "King-size" bed was a manger.

The thinking that caused the problem can't be used to solve the problem,

You are never too big to do the little things.

God can redefine what we consider to be impossible.

The biggest question is not how we can live longer, but how we can live better.

Be prepared. If you need a parachute and don't have one, you won't need one again.

Growing old is inevitable-growing smarter is optional.

Do the things God created you to do and avoid the things that God told you not to do.

Our task is not to get God on our side, but for us to get on God's side.

God didn't come to take sides-He came to take over.

Until you change your thinking, you will only have re-runs of the past.

The game of life is not baseball. In life three strikes and you're not out. Never give up. Never quit. At age 89, I live this principle every day. - Lt. Gen. Hal G. Moore.

"Well Done" is for good and faithful servants-not steaks. Derric Johnson

You never know what church service will impact and change your life, but it won't be the one you missed. Derric Johnson

If you can't fly, run. If you can't run, walk. If you can't walk, crawl. But by all means keep moving. Martin Luther King

Aim at Heaven and you will get earth "thrown in." Aim at earth and you will get neither. C. S. Lewis

HOW FINANCES WILL BE USED

- All honorariums and gifts received for preaching/teaching services offered by John Ed will go to the budget of the John Ed Mathison Leadership Ministries and will be used in the following ways.

- To fund the cost of developing and implementing seminars and training events.

- To give scholarships to younger pastors who might not be able to afford some of the seminars in the United States.

- To help fund other seminar/Conference opportunities for pastors.

- To cover expenses when participating in training opportunities for pastors in other nations. Some of these will attract 3,000 pastors, and many of them will need financial assistance.

- To cover office and administrative expenses for the ministry.

- To fund and expand our digital ministry reaching thousands each week.

HOW TO MAKE TAX DEDUCTIBLE FINANCIAL CONTRIBUTIONS

Contributions by cash, check, credit card, etc.

To contribute by credit card you can text JOHNED to 51555 or visit our website (johnedmathison.org), select the "Support & Giving" tab, then click "Donate."

• Checks should be mailed to:

John Ed Mathison Leadership Ministries
4135 Carmichael Road | Suite 3000
Montgomery, AL 36106

• Designation from a Charitable Foundation

Your Role in the Future

SUPPORT this ministry financially. Future ministry opportunities will require more financial investment. This ministry will be fiscally responsible—but we will not make initial decisions for ministry opportunities based on what it will cost. If God is in it—it will be supported. If it is not supported—we will rethink and redirect our available resources. Your financial support is critical for our future ministry.

SHARE the daily Got a Minute audio messages, weekly Got a Minute video message, daily Good News video, weekly blogs and monthly Go Getters & Go Givers Podcast with your friends and business associates.

PRAY bodaciously and expectantly for this ministry! "The sincere prayer of a Godly person has great power and produces wonderful results." (James 5:16)

www.ingramcontent.com/pod-product-compliance
Lightning Source LLC
Chambersburg PA
CBHW051219120626
46547CB00013B/1417